MW00603715

The Heart of a Traveler

The Heart of a Traveler

REFLECTIONS FROM THE FATHOMLESS EDGE OF THE WORLD

ARI MARSH

PhantaSea Books
Honolulu, Hawaii

THE HEART OF A TRAVELER:
Reflections from the Fathomless Edge of the World
ARI MARSH
Copyright © 2017 by Ari Marsh
All rights reserved.
Published by PhantaSea Books, Honolulu, Hawaii

ISBN: 0692832866
ISBN 13: 9780692832868
Library of Congress Control Number: 2017931290
PhantaSea Books, Honolulu, HI

Cover photo: Shadow Self in the Crystal Fields, a self-portrait, version one, Central Baja California, Mexico, overlooking the Sea of Cortez. Photo by Ari Marsh.

All text and photographic images included herein are subject to the laws of copyright protection and may not be reproduced, copied, printed, or manipulated in any way without prior written consent from the author or photographer. All rights reserved.

Other Titles by

ARI MARSH

Smiling at the Sun: Ways of the Golden Path
Soul Rider Publications, 1991

The Soul Rider: A Surfer's Perspective of the World
Soul Rider Publications, 1992

The Voice of Eternity: A Book of Aphorisms
Soul Rider Publications, 1993

Soul Rider II: Neptune's Dream
Further Perspectives on the Surfers' World
Soul Rider Publications, 1995

Sea-Soaked Heart (Soul Rider III): Thoughts from the Pacific Coast
Soul Rider Publications, 2004

Echoes from the Sun: A Modern Quest for the Fountain of Youth
PhantaSea Books, 2012
Available in paperback and Kindle through Amazon.com
and other retailers.
www.echoesfromthesun.com

www.AriMarsh.com

Contents

Dedications

The Heart of a Traveler: Reflections from the Fathomless Edge of the World is in part dedicated to a select group of extraordinary people in my life who have encouraged me to write, follow my own individual path, and both practice and produce my art, which is primarily music and writing. Endless gratitude, love, and sincere appreciation to you all... to my parents, Robert and Kerstin, who have patiently and tirelessly loved and encouraged me, even amidst my most impractical, non-traditional life choices, as well as through my darkest hours; and for the inspiring examples you have provided me by being such loving, generous, and compassionate human beings... to my life-long friend and brother, Eric Holland, for a truly enduring friendship built around respect, love, incredible surfing adventures, ridiculous laughter, and sincere appreciation for one another in spite of the physical distances that have often been between us... to Dario Berrini for true friendship, and for the countless hundreds of hours we have spent immersed in deep conversation and meaningful discussion; and for always being a detailed, honest critic of my work... to my dear bro, Tony Lasley, for soulful, kava-induced music, deep friendship, inspiring Beatles conversations, and for sharing in the mutual Ben-like living of which few can truly understand... to David Nandan Powell for all the years of music, jamming, performing, creating, and supporting one another in our various musical endeavors, always with the focus of spirituality and more healthy, enlightened living... to the Brothers of the Ranch: Jorge Tuma, Ted Tillinghast, and Randall Hayward, for decades of friendship, openness, and honesty, often in the midst of challenging personal transformations; and for the sharing of powerful insights related to growth, change, and mutual evolution along the spiritual pathway of the Hero's Journey... and to my traveling, surfing, writer-musician buddy from the days of old, Quinn Haber, for his assistance in bringing this work to publication.

Acknowledgements

To all of you who have been an Other in my life, who have influenced this work in some way through your presence, the journeys we have shared, and perhaps the love, joy, friendship, laughter, grief, or heartbreak that we have brought to one another's lives due to our paths crossing... Thank you for being a part of my journey... Linda Lobbestael, Traci Dinwiddie, Nicole Wedick, Soren Mitchell, Steve Hodge, Jason Appleton, Michael Neustein, Jason Weber, Richard "Ben" Benson, Deanna Cross, Darlene Medve, Hanna Nogiec, Selina Doran, Lisa Ezzard, Bahman Sarram, Ian Marsh, John Wirtz, Chris Dunn, William Wagner, Christian Jensen, Vince Doran, Christopher Smith, Uta Hughey, Rebecca Short, Elissa Blount, Keith Noel, Jennifer M. Benivue, Jane Lido, Uhane Moore, Anessa Palisadia, Amy Liszt, Madeline Wardbergh, Annette Monterosso, Lauri Robbins Ericson, Christy Ahna Zahava, Katie Freiling, Komala Saunders, Rachael Johnson, Brahman Kyrie Shanti, Michelle N. Chapman, Suzanne Palmer, Rose Tan, Kristin Cooper-Gulak, Tiffany Reece, Cameron Calder, Carol Eliel, Jason and Pia Rotman, Whitney Kear, Gabriela Flores, Mary Froemke, Kris Wallace DeGrazio, Jen Satya Peters, Cat Delena, Krista Richards, Jess Johnson, Alicia Diaz, Courtney Acamo, Lauren Wilson, Laurel Madeline, Aimee Isabel, Kathleen Moscato, Melinda Nevins, Kirk Van Allyn, Charles Kovatch, Jaime Berndt, Joshua Alvord, David Patri of Seaweed & Gravel, James "Haggo" Haggard, David Defoe, Donald Stacey, Jim Cowing, Tony Rosaci, Santo Rosaci, Victor Kiklowicz, Rick Merritt, LeRoy Foster, Bruno Rota, Pat Kiklowicz, Sandra Stacey, Sarah Alexander, Andrea Graber, Doug DeStefano, Robert Hensley, Lamine Thiam, Frank Lazzaro, Jack Lampl, Bill M., Rachel Leshaw, Denise Reppenhagen, Christina Jones, Suzanne Forbes-Vierling, Hilary and Sundaram La Pierre, Kamlesh Singh, Michael Joseph Ferguson, Prem Thierry Maurel, Maitreya Shanti, Kevin Dalfonzo, Dave Erickson, Lorena Nunes, James Aplington, Rick Ireton, Nayan Banerjee, Grace Jin Kim, Perry Smith, Darcy Jones, Chandra Lynne, Christie Perry, Alan and Holly Hubbard, Terri Craft and Dan Levy of Juice Magazine,

Keith Sharp, Dale Pigford, Brian Rioux, Julie Bordo, Jennifer Best, Stacie Krajchir-Tom, Sue Reynolds, Susie Shaughnessy, Randy Troy, Brady Young, Dr. Richard Carpenter, Matthew Sonken, Gary Taylor, Thierry Chatelain, Buck Holland, Rodney Moss, Charles Magel, Martin, Mary Volz, all my relatives in the Marsh, Claesson, Hughey, Thunelius, and Hadley families, and so many others...

Photographic Contributions

While the majority of the photographs included in *The Heart of a Traveler* belong to the author, select images, as noted within the text, were contributed by the following photographers (in order of appearance): Dario Berrini, Randall Hayward, Linda Lobbestael, Mike Barnes, and Jim Cowing. On behalf of Ari Marsh and PhantaSea Books, thank you for your artistic contribution.

Leucadia, California

To the various unique and interesting Leucadia surfers with whom I have shared countless surf sessions throughout the many years since my arrival at Beacon's Beach more than 25 years ago in 1991, including John Wirtz, Bill Parker, Jerry St. John, Robert Saxton, Andy Poff and sons Alex and Ian, Brandon Williams, Mike Foreman, Micky Maga, David Ash, Dave Clark, Peter Sprague, Gary Hanel, T.J., Larry (who moved to Hawaii), Miles Bender, Kahuna Bob Edwards, Jason Weber, brothers Greg and Chris Puha, Jeff Lueras, the Unsworth family, Brett Stewart, Doug Jopes, brothers Mike and Gary Beecher, the one and only Kit Horn, and many others who have come and gone over the years... Thanks and aloha! It's been a great ride!

Humanitarian and Spiritual Leaders

To the various guides of humanity, the dispellers of ignorance and darkness, without whom this world would be lost: His Holiness the Fourteenth Dalai Lama, Mata Amritanandamayi Devi, Mahatma Gandhi, Dr. Martin Luther King, Jr., Nelson Mandela, Jelaluddin Rumi, Meher Baba, Robert Nesta "Bob" Marley, Ramana Maharshi, Paramahansa Yogananda, and so many others... Thank you. I honor you all and bow before you with the deepest of respect.

Tribute to the Native Elders

To several of the great elders of humanity who I consider our wisest warrior ancestors... you who have walked this continent and traveled this path long before me... especially the great tribal leader of the Hunkpapa Teton band of the Lakota Sioux, Tatanka-Iyotanka, also known as Sitting Bull; and the great tribal leader of the Nez Perce, Hinmaton-Yalatkit, whose name means Thunder Rolling Down the Mountain, also known as Chief Joseph; and Hehaka-Sapa, Black Elk, the great holy man of the Oglala Sioux... Thank you for the guidance and wisdom with which you have provided me in this life through the examples of your own lives. I feel your strength and inspiration with me at all times, and I dare say, I empathize with your deep grief, and the loss that is so much a part of this earthly journey. Though I am not a part of your biological lineage, I believe that we are connected in the mysterious realm of spirit and soul. Our sufferings are one, our tears are one, as are our fierce, courageous shouts of joy and celebration, and our love for the land. Our hearts are one, great elders of humanity.

Introduction

T he following poems, writings, stories, and letters were written by the author throughout a broad period ranging from 1991-2017. Some of the work reflects extended time spent in quiet observation, whether engaged in the exploration of nature or floating about on a surfboard in the ocean. For much of the 1990s, the author journeyed regularly, often alone, to the remote deserts and isolated seacoasts of Baja California, Mexico, in order to surf, hike, and write in virtual seclusion. The mid-90s, specifically, was a period where the author delved deepest into his own inner nature. Again, it was quite often from the vantage point of the ocean, whereupon he rode countless thousands of waves and carefully examined his personal relationship to the natural and oceanic world. Throughout the years 1993-2004, the author traveled to some twenty countries throughout Europe, Asia, and South America, both as a student of life, culture, and spirituality, and as a sort of wandering explorer. Much of the work included in *The Heart of a Traveler* reflects his unique explorations in searching the world, both within and without, for personal meaning and insight into the purpose of life itself.

Prologue:
The Fathomless Edge of the World

~⟶⟳

The Edge. The word *edge* can be defined in a variety of ways. It is *a line or border at which an object, area, or surface begins or ends, such as the edge of a road*; it is *a brink or verge*; *a point near the beginning or the end, such as the edge of disaster*; it is *the threshold of danger or ruin, as in living on the edge* (Merriam-Webster; Random House). In the context of *The Heart of a Traveler: Reflections from the Fathomless Edge of the World*, the Edge is a very physical place, as in the western edge of the North American continent, the seacoasts of California and Mexico—regions of which I am quite familiar. The Edge is the beginning of the ocean, where land falls into sea, where solid becomes liquid, where familiar becomes unfamiliar… where the norms and customs of culture cease, where Manifest Destiny slips away into that which is unconquerable, where civilization ends and mystery and imagination begin.

The Edge is also a perspective, an observational point of view, thus being the specific outlook of one who abides outside the confines of traditional society, on the far fringes of normalcy, on the peripheries of that which is knowable and definable. The Edge is where common reality blurs into strangeness. Accordingly, the perspective from the Edge is one of indefinite possibilities.

There are those amongst humanity whose very existence or identity is dependent upon their active relationship with the Edge, with the natural world and the wild places of Earth. These are the explorers, the adventurers, the artists, the philosophers, the sailors, the surfers, the mountaineers, the wanderers, the dreamers. Such individuals may appear to exist outside the realm of common society, for the focus of their lives may be at some distant point far beyond the social world. Thus, the Edge in its completeness, is a lifestyle.

As we are beings of body, mind, heart, and spirit, the Edge in its ultimate form is both experienced and felt. We feel the Edge when we realize our fragility, the fleeting nature of our physical lives. Though in realizing this vulnerability, this mortality, we glimpse something beyond ourselves, our direct relationship to that which will outlive us—the living planet Earth, its tremendous mountains, lush forests, deep canyons, flowing rivers, unfathomable oceans... its barren moon and the celestial tapestries of gaseous planets and glimmering stars which float in silence throughout the incomprehensible vastness of the cosmos.

When we realize our true oneness with all things in existence, we begin to bridge the gap between mortality and immortality. This conscious bridging, this dual subtraction and expansion of self, this realization of our own transcendent beingness, is the very essence and heart of the Edge. This perspective is, in actuality, a coming into the center of one's existence. Thus to fully experience the Edge is ultimately to abide in the center of one's own being, whereupon we love, laugh, cry, dream, create, and *feel*.

Although this state of being is in truth more of a centered point from which to live our lives, it is not the perspective from which the majority of us see the world on a daily basis. In fact, viewing our individual lives in this manner of profound interconnectedness is often completely foreign to us and at odds with the majority of our daily social interactions and behaviors. Thus, until the modern cultures of the world experience a dramatic shift in values, this uncommon perspective on our own lives and our relationship to the Universe will continue to be known as the Edge.

Through *The Heart of a Traveler*, I invite the reader to explore his or her own relationship to the Edge, to embark upon curious journeys to the foreign outposts of consciousness. Nothing about the reality that we are experiencing is concrete. There is no up, there is no down. This Earth, may I remind you, is a spinning globe revolving around our sun—a massive, flaming, spherical nucleic inferno—at a speed of approximately 67,000 miles per hour... all of which, in total, is a mere speck of dust in a truly immense, brilliant galaxy flying and whirling through an infinite, mysterious Universe.

In actuality, we are all on the Edge, although few of us realize it. We are soaring at galactic speeds... and our lives are merely a brief flash of energy, light, and consciousness—an ephemeral radiance.

There are seven basic principles to life on the Edge, and they are as follows:

1. You are not safe.
2. The true natural world is wild and untamed.
3. Life is fleeting and your physical self will die.
4. The Universe is vast, incredible, and incomprehensible.
5. You are a conscious, living being in an unknown land.
6. Love exists; deep connections with other living and non-living entities are possible and real.
7. In this love and connectedness, you are entirely safe—even unto physical death.

Ari J. Marsh, Leucadia, California, 2017

Part One

Trace Bands of Solar Light

Trace Bands of Solar Light:
A Study in Self-Dissolution, the Quaking Earth, and Northern California Magic

An earthquake shook the San Diego coastline this afternoon. Though mild, it was enough to wake most of us up for a moment and remind us that we live on a planet, are part of an ecosystem, and are bound by powerful natural forces that are ultimately untamable and beyond our control. We stopped for a minute, most of us anyway, and remembered for a few brief seconds that we are small and fragile beings, that we don't really own anything—not even our own lives—and that the safety and security which we daily convince ourselves that we possess is but an illusion.

The shaking hurled a fist-sized quartz crystal from a shelf in my living room and tossed it onto the floor. It also toppled a framed photograph of a buddy and me from a surfing trip to a point break deep in Baja California. I stood quietly in the aftermath of this subtle quake on this summer afternoon... thinking... reflecting... wondering...

I had recently returned from a six-week, summer journey camping, surfing, hiking, and visiting good friends throughout Central and Northern California. I had spent a handful of days camping alone along the Big Sur coast. With virtually no commitments and a wide-open time frame, I had dropped into what I call the state of dissolution, where much of the ideas that occupy our daily lives and realities begin to dissolve. Dissolution meaning *the act or process of dissolving, as in decay, disintegration, or even death* (Merriam-Webster), and thus the state of dissolution, to me, is something that can be experienced when one departs from his or her daily routine or normal life for a duration of time that allows one to distance him or her self from the feelings, concepts, demands, responsibilities, and expectations that define his or her personality, identity, and sense of self. Often, it is in this mental state where profound insights can be realized or previously inaccessible creativity can be accessed. While in Big Sur, I had temporarily forgotten what day of the week or month it was, and my seemingly endless list of To Do's became meaningless. I had moments of being completely lost to the concepts of "who I am" and "what I do"... moments where identity dissolved into glorious sunset colors on mountain hikes or along unnamed, forgotten stretches of coastline... but always something drew me back.

After Big Sur, I headed north to connect with two very close friends, Eric Holland and Steve Hodge, both lifelong surfers. We rendezvoused at Steve's property north of the Golden Gate in a rural, mountainous coastal town that I have promised to keep anonymous. Steve owns a plot of land and lives in a small solar-powered home that he built himself. From his place, we drove dirt roads through the coastal mountains to reach narrow footpaths once trod by the Miwok native people. These secret paths led to extremely isolated beaches seldom visited by outsiders. Comparatively, this is nothing like the San Diego coastline. There is no Del Mar, no La Jolla, no Encinitas... no multi-million dollar homes with ocean views, no BMW's, no outdoor cafes, no surf shops, no Whole Foods, no gyms, no bars, no yoga studios, no burger joints, no 7-Elevens, no smoothies, and cell phone service is virtually nonexistent. However, in spite of the tremendous natural beauty, the area can be quite daunting for there is very little sunshine, at least in the summer months, and thus there is no glistening, turquoise water nor emerald-colored waves to be found.

This is a stretch of coast where turkey vultures hover over uninviting, rocky beaches and feed on decomposing fish... where cold, gray mist and fog block out sunshine for days and weeks on end... where fierce north winds blow through the coastal forests. The footpaths and dirt trails are lined with poison oak, which the Miwok developed an immunity to by apparently ingesting minute amounts over long periods of time. If one does finally reach these lost coves and beaches, the waves are definitely not playful.

Surfing along this wild coastline is more often about survival than anything else. It's about making peace with the cold, the elements, and one's own momentary insignificance. Beyond that, surfing is about surrendering—if at all possible—to the fear in one's gut, the fear of the great white shark, whom the local fishermen, sailors, and surfers refer to as "the Landlord." The threat is indeed real, and the part of one's self that is still primal can feel it within. Entering into the ocean in these parts demands we come to terms with the idea and reality that we are not unconquerable human beings, but potential prey to natural forces and marine life beyond our scope and control.

Steve was in the water when a major attack occurred several years ago. He was fifteen feet away when the Landlord surfaced with ferocious, Amtrak-style power and grabbed another surfer by the torso and pulled him down, jaws and teeth snapping.

"This is something you never forget," he told me, "something that causes you to wake up in the middle of the night in a panic... heart thumping... drenched in sweat."

These are the stories that surfers share up here, as if to help keep one another aware and on guard. Surfing in this region has nothing to do with flip-flops and Jack Johnson music. It's about five millimeter wetsuits, hoods, booties, and breathing through your fears while fog banks collide with mountains. It's about pondering an ocean, a world, a vastness that, at times, can be terrifyingly dark, cold, heavy, and lonely.

But there's another side to it, something very mystical and tough to put into words. It has to do with a delicate and nebulous truth about being alive on this planet only for a short time... about the temporary, fleeting nature of our lives and our loved ones... about becoming, once again, part of the mystery of natural life. It's about entering a space, both physically and psychologically, where social constructs and media-driven realities are meaningless. It's about tapping into the source, the nature within and around us, and becoming part of something incomprehensibly beautiful and wondrous.

Over the days that followed, we surfed two spots, simply known as the Point and the Rock. Large southern hemisphere and northwest swells combined to rock the coast. The waves were big—really challenging—and the take-off spots were lined with huge, jagged rocks... truly intense! And although I emerged in one piece physically—save for a few moderately bruised ribs—emotionally and perhaps spiritually I'd been blown apart and scattered amongst the ancient land, vast sky, and fathomless sea...

I picked up the quartz crystal from the floor and held it in my hand for a moment before returning it to the shelf. As for the friend and fellow surfer who stood beside me in the framed photograph that had also been toppled by the quake, it was Eric Holland.

Although the language or languages that nature speaks can be quite vague by our standards, and her messages are often ambiguous at best, I figured I'd listen and attempt to interpret… and as I stood there, what I gathered from the moment was this… *Go down to the ocean. Right now. Shift perspective. TAP IN. Rediscover who you are, or at the very least, remember who you are not.*

With that I grabbed a classic, 1970s, seven-foot surfboard from the corner of my living room. It's a faded yellow single-fin shaped by the legendary surfer and waterman, Dick Brewer. I acquired it nearly twenty years ago at a surf shop down the street in Leucadia, the northern part of Encinitas, where I've lived for many years. I sauntered out the door to begin a brisk, short walk to the beach. One of my neighbors was standing outside as I approached.

"Did you feel that earthquake?" she asked concernedly.

"I did," I answered.

"I hope it's not a foreshock," she said. Most people who are familiar with earthquakes know that smaller quakes called foreshocks commonly precede larger seismic events.

"Hope not, Katie," I responded simply.

"Scientists say we're due for a big one!" she called as I crossed the street and hit the railroad tracks that parallel Pacific Coast Highway. She was scared, I could feel it.

The beach was once again shrouded in a thick, gray marine layer. We've had weeks without even a slight peek of sun, as if some post-apocalyptic fallout has blotted out the light. Gray ocean, amidst darker gray sky… feels more like winter than summer… feels more like Northern than Southern California. But there is a glimpse of hope, of promise, for trace bands of solar light were visible this afternoon at the distant horizon.

And so in the aftermath of the quake, I surfed the fading south swell. Still stoked, as always, to get in the ocean, TAP IN, and feel the glide. The pelicans were soaring, seemingly undisturbed by both the lack of sun and the quaking earth. They just went on in streamlined flight… dignified, harmonized… without any visible hint or sign of their fragile nature and delicate vulnerability.

Shadow Selves of Eric Holland and Ari Marsh, coastal Central
Baja California, Mexico. Photo by the author.

Part Two

Sea-Soaked Heart

Sea-Soaked Heart

I am forever wandering these shores…
roaming the fluid edges of the world,
gliding beside the rust-colored cliffs
with the pelicans.

I am forever wandering the misty, salt-laden lands of liquid…
my heart soaked with sea water,
my mind bleached with years of golden sun.
I spin and roam
alongside this sacred, bejeweled sea,
my head dizzy with ocean fragrance.

I am forever wandering these ancient shores…
my feet, shoeless and tough,
the cuts on my toes bleed blue.
My ears, plugged with sand and salt,
remind me of distant sorrows
long washed away by the sea.

I am forever wandering…
wandering…
lit with the bluest of all splendors,
alive
with the delightful taste of salt upon my lips.

Twilight from 27,000 Feet

Deep bands of molten gold
and flaming orange
hover at the horizon
in stark contrast to the dark silhouette of earth.
Sprawling mountains and townships
nearly disappear into the vast expanse of continent.
Seen from above
all appears so small and insignificant,
almost meaningless…

The horizon is ablaze…
burning with the gleaming afterglow
of the vanished sun…
but only for a moment
for the embers of the burnt day
only briefly whisper
and softly hiss.

Just above the smoldering, fiery glow
colors brighten into soft yellows
even brilliant turquoise blues and greens…
Stretching higher, above the horizon
the luminous hues of sunset smear
and fade
into the dark, fathomless depths
of the encroaching night.

Behold this twilight
this brief interlude betwixt day and night
this marvelous earth

the ever-changing spectacles of day and night
of spinning planet circling immense sun
of spiraling solar system whirling through vast, unknown, starlit galaxy…

Where are we, I wonder.
Strange land
yet familiar,
so vividly familiar somewhere deep within myself.
I am those burning embers,
the glowing ash of day
of life
of sun
of flame…
and yet
I am the dark, colorless silhouette
of barren land
of vast cosmos
of brief twinkling star
some billion eons away…
always mysterious
unreachable
alone…

The horizon's colors have faded now,
sunset has gone elsewhere
to other lands
to other days and nights…
The night rules all now
its mantle of blue midnight
spreads across this thousand-mile continent
overpowering even bustling supercenters of electric lights
of twenty-four hour madness
if we only allow it to…
if we only surrender ourselves

to the enduring truth of this amazing mystery
of frothing oceans
of whirling spheres and exploding suns
of brief floating specks of interstellar dust
and the finite
fleeting
delicate pulse
of our own hearts...

--Heading east from California via commercial jet, April 2006

Punta Canoas: The Ends of the Earth

To the ends of the earth we have come,
where the prehistoric land
and tall, barren mountains
crumble into the fathomless sea.
Humans dwell here not,
for harshness thrives.
With eternity's ever-present patience
the flaming sun scorches the landscape,
sucking it of its moisture,
making it void of life.

The sea, blue and cold,
crashes against the steep cliffs
and calls the brittle earth back unto itself.
Cracking lifelessly,
rocks fall hundreds of feet
as the dry earth collapses
unable to resist the ocean's mighty call.
Pebbles crumble and rocks tumble
as mountains fall into the sea,
soon to become sand.

These are the ends of the earth.
But be deceived not,
for the dry, sweltering earth lives.
The prehistoric earth lives.
And it is here that I find my home.
Beside the fearless ocean and sheer cliffs I abide,

knowing that I, like the crumbling, ancient land,
too shall be claimed by sea.

And so I, like the cracking earth,
lay naked and bare
and play host to nobody.
For I too shall fall wholeheartedly
into the deep, vast womb of sea
and return to that from whence I came.

--Punta Canoas, Baja California, Mexico, 1996

Unspoiled, untainted, undeveloped, uninhabited… and thus original, natural, raw, and wild… a stretch of Baja California's Lost Coast. Photo by the author.

Pelican Wing

The silent rising and falling of a passing swell...
The deep golden light of the sinking sun...
Crisp ocean air, brisk and fresh...
Heartbeat, pulse, tidal flow...

What is this mystery and beauty,
this blend of liquid and earth, vapor and light,
to which we belong?

An inhalation, an exhalation, the lift of wave...
Rising to my feet, body upon board,
board upon wave, wave sculpted by wind...
All of it—all of us—traversing ocean, as planet circling sun,
as sun floating and drifting through—through where?

Movement, motion, speed, glide... and yet stillness...
Vast, incomprehensible stillness...
Where action is actionless, and ultimate motion motionless.

Now, here, she approaches me in streamlined flight...
A brush of air upon my face...
A waft of wind from a pelican's wing.

--North Beacon's, Leucadia, California, Planet Earth, November 5, 2012

A Glimpse into Night Surfing

I've been night surfing the past three evenings, from sunset into the first two hours of darkness. Dolphins have visited me each time in the twilight. I've studied the stars from the water and watched Venus set below the western horizon while bright green, shimmering, bioluminescent radiance has lit up the dark waves around me. It's been astounding! Surfing in the darkness has forced me to understand waves with new sensitivities... like interpreting the speed of the ride by tuning into the sensation of water rushing underneath my board... and determining wave steepness by the way reflections of light from land bend upon the dark wave surfaces beyond me. So much to experience—to tap into—in this amazing land, if we have the courage and creativity to explore new possibilities, and different ways of doing that which we've done so many times before...

--South Beacon's, Leucadia, California, September 2010

A Rendezvous with Chaos

405 freeway northbound, coming into Los Angeles
Rush hour, 1991

Upon arrival to the city
I was greeted by masses of cars
all going nowhere slowly.
Horrendous traffic
spawned impatience and anger.
Eyes turned red
brows stiffened and mouths tightened
as if in battle.
Clean, everyday citizens
became hideous,
fighting with one another to pull ahead,
to arrive at the next freeway exit
some ten seconds before someone else.
The aggressiveness
and lack of cooperation
was so terribly apparent to me,
though to others it seemed commonplace, perhaps even natural.
After the third person tailgated me, blew his horn,
and flipped me off as he sped around me,
I began to lose myself and join the madness.
Angry eyes beckoned me
clenched fists challenged me
unhappy hearts clawed at me
pulling me into chaos.
As the last threads of my sanity were unraveling
and a monstrous force within me began to explode
a California brown pelican glided up beside the freeway,
flew parallel with my truck for some ten yards,

then soared high, crossing west toward the setting sun
far beyond the reach of rush hour traffic.
I exhaled,
pausing to watch the fiery sun
and the pelican riding the updrafts toward the coast.
Saved again by the sea...
I must remember who I am, I thought,
and not allow myself to become the insanity that surrounds me.
I will accept not the hellish beckoning of those around me,
but rather the peaceful challenge of the pelican.

More Musings from the Freeways of L.A.
Late spring, 2013

Meandering through the freeways of Los Angeles... the arterial system of the city... endlessly moving, never quiet, never still... always the rush of travel, the comings and goings of the city's inhabitants... like cells whirling through a cosmic bloodstream. I notice the endless array of billboards and advertising signs. Everywhere something is being sold. Seemingly everything in this culture has become about money—having it, earning it, getting more of it—so you can have more things, acquire more possessions. Never is enough, enough. It's as if a silent, hypnotic mantra is ringing out endlessly, everywhere we look, instructing each citizen to perform his or her most vital social action and "buy... buy... buy... buy..." Have we collectively devolved into mere robotic consumers?

Imagine... if the advertising signs and billboards were not the end result of a society based upon extreme capitalism, excess materialism, and ever-increasing profits, but one based upon mutual cooperation, environmental appreciation, natural wisdom... love... even shared participation in one another's well-being. Imagine... if all these billboards selling products that we really don't need in the first place were suddenly replaced with inspirational reminders, such as:

"Honor the Earth!"

"Respect one another."

"Breathe deep."

"Be here now."

"Love to all beings."

"Om, shanti, peace..."

What would that world look like?

Shh

Shh. Wait.
Listen. Lisssten.
A soft ring hums through the skies.
The breath of the cosmos faintly whispers to us.
Open up, my friend,
but not your ears.
Look deeply,
but not with your eyes…
with your soul, my friend,
your soul.
The everlasting blast of the universe
shivers through our cells.
Its radiance pours its love
into the vase of our beings.
Its wisdom waters the dormant buds
of our tomorrow.
Quench your thirst with love from the source
and let your heart sing
to those who come from beyond.

Shh. Wait.
Lisssten.
A soft voice speaks through the clouds.
The sound of nature sighs in the growing grass.
A twinkling eye beckons to us
in the garden's misty dew.
Hold your thoughts, my friend,
the elusive voice of the cosmos

calls to us now.
"I am… I am… I am…"
Its message is clear.
The time is now.

The Whisper

Whisper
deeply, gently, softly,
wordlessly speaks the breath of life.
Across vast oceans the sound has come
to meet the sea-polished rocks of the shoreline
and the powdery, white dunes.
Open me mine ears,
behold life's caress.
Onward travels the whisper
smoothly, evenly, unceasingly,
as the breeze takes it to the tall mountains,
to the grassy meadows and forests of pine
graced with sighing brooks,
to the thin, pure air and crystal skies.
Behold! The sound speaks in the stillness.
Know I the whisper, know I the sound,
so I am there too.
Everywhere, all encompassing, forever
is the whisper.
Listen
deeply
and you shall know it.

--Sierra San Pedro Mártir, Baja California, Mexico, 1995

Fusion

My thoughts flow into the sea of humanity
as ripples across the water,
as streaks across the wave
carved by my sharp fins.

My thoughts flow into the sea of humanity
as soft spray blown into the air
by stiff offshore winds,
as beads of whitewater hurled by a light purple rail
across a backdrop of blue wave.
My thoughts caress like a hand
upon the smooth face of a wave.

Like my thoughts—my words,
the ripples—the waves
disperse into the vast sea.
But they never really disappear,
they never cease.
They are merely absorbed,
fused,
into one
with the precious whole.

--1994

Miracles

Miracles, miracles, miracles
everywhere to behold
but you've got to leave your house
you've got to get off your couch.
GO!
Get up and see the world.
Explore.
Live.
Breathe.
BE.

--Malibu, California, 2001

Impact

One week after the San Diego wildfires, October 1996

Today the sun shines brilliantly and the California sky is blue and clear. The day is pristine, and though it is quite warm, the air is crisp and fresh. The ocean is alive, glistening with diamond-shining beads of sunlight on its crystal blue surface. The nearby hills are blackened, dusted with ash and charcoal. Hawks soar above the barren land searching futilely for mice and rodents. Ecosystems are destroyed; natural cycles broken. Those who have survived the wildfires (including the dozens of now homeless people) have been forced to relocate. Some head west, toward the coast, while others go inland, deeper into the brush in search of areas that have remained unscathed.

Turkey vultures, several of them, soar further west than I have ever seen. Their black feathers starkly contrast with the deep blue of sky as they glide to the coast in search of food. Their presence agitates the crows, who become defensive and reckless. The seagulls group closer together; their circles tighten. Pelicans, however, pay no attention; poised and graceful, they continue their streamlined flights up and down the coast.

A raccoon lay dead in the street. Forced from his habitat by flame and smoke, he fled west toward the unruly clatter of El Camino Real Highway and its barrage of automobiles. He met his end trying to cross a stretch of surface unfamiliar to his sharp claws—concrete. Just beyond him was the promised land—unscathed coastal foothills.

Over the hills, a shimmering blue-green wall of water approaches the beach. It raises up, doubling its height as it reaches the shallow, sandy shoreline. A lone surfer paddles into it. Smiling, he jumps to his feet. His hair blows back into the warm breeze as he skims across the dazzling, liquid blue glass.

Up the beach, the same wave crashes upon an empty stretch of coast. Shattering the silence, it explodes into an infinity of tiny globules of white foam. It vanishes quickly, leaving the rocks and sand glistening with moisture.

An inland hawk sits atop the bluff surveying his newly found coastal habitat. A few sandpipers scurry up the beach, avoiding the next approaching wave. Reality fades into the soft hiss of the incoming tide. Sizzling ripples of golden sunshine track across the vast ocean to the horizon. There, the silken sun falls off the edge of the world and slips into eternity...

--Encinitas, California

The Winged Horse

There was a winged horse in the sky tonight...
It stretched forth into surreality
from the grand spectacle of sunset.
As my beloved Pacific and I met again
after many months
the golden rays from the dropping sun
blazed a deep orange into the early-evening clouds.
I sat,
floating on my board
watching...
It was insane
really.
The ocean moved slowly...
time grinded to a halt
as the sun hovered in molten gold.
I turned, caught a wave,
stood up and glided across the beach
while the moving waters danced beneath my feet and board,
and the colors of sunset deepened.
I paddled back out
and again found the winged horse in the sky.
It flamed in pink now
above the horizon.
Clouds stretched further into the western sky.
The ocean was smooth
like a sheet of liquid glass,
and ribbons of sunlight flashed mesmerizingly around me.
Is this even real, I wondered?
How could it be?
Beyond the horse, I noticed another figure...

an angel.
As I watched in awe
this fiery angel breathed in the sunset
and then exhaled a plume of smoke from its mouth.
The plume rose high into orange and purple hues.
I turned and caught another wave,
a long left.
Again I glided across the beach
back arched
arms outstretched in soulful Christ pose...
It brought me to the shore.
When I turned to look back at the western sky,
the sun had at last gone,
the angel and the winged horse too...
all had vanished...
Colors darkened into twilight as night approached.
I made my way across the sand and up the tall bluffs...

--San Onofre, California, November 2003

Sunset... Reflections on Windows and Minds

The orange glow of sunset
lights up the west-facing windows
of a single house on a solitary hillside
in the Malibu canyons.
Its residents meander from room to room
preparing for the steadily approaching night.
I watch from atop the summit of a nearby peak,
breathless from a vigorous hike.
The fragrant sages and chaparral surround me.

The house vanishes before me
as the deepening shine
of the reflected sunset upon its windows intensifies
and expands.
The brilliant glow lasts only a few minutes,
eight, maybe ten,
and then it fades
as the sun slips behind the sea
into darkness.

Sunset
now
is happening a few miles further to the west.
Somewhere over the Pacific
the sun falls,
casting its glow upon smooth, shimmering waters.
Soaring sea birds
and passing sailors

gazing into the broad sky from the loneliness of their ships
behold its glorious colors—
its serenity,
however brief.

Hours later, the sun is still setting.
Now it is happening over the western shore of the big island of Hawaii.
Local residents stop...
their tasks and conversations—
their comings and goings—
cease
for a time
as they watch and think.
Their troubles, for the moment,
do not exist
as they look to the sky in wonder.

Continuing its westward transit over the planet,
the sun falls before virtually unknown islands
in the Mid-Pacific.
They lay
sealed in the grand solitude
and blue depths of the ocean.

Further...
further west...
the sun continues to traverse the sky.
The Earth continues in its orbit
and revolves upon its own axis,
ever turning both towards and away from the sun.
Now, finally, the golden sun rises
over the eastern shore of New Zealand...

crosses Africa...
and later breaks dawn
over the eastern shore of the United States,
illumining the fiery green, coastal waters
of the Atlantic.
Somehow, it seems
only a moment ago it left my sight
yet it will soon again set
beyond the coastal hills of California.

Constantly
simultaneously
rising
and setting
from the vantage point of one or another—
be it bird or sailor,
casual observer or troubled soul.
Every moment
every instant
is one to behold—
a glorious sunrise,
a never before experienced sunset.
All day long...
all night long...
sunrises
and sunsets.

Right now, as you read this,
somewhere—
maybe nearby
or perhaps in a remote and exotic land
the sun is setting,

and simultaneously
elsewhere
on the other side of the globe
it is rising before awakening eyes.

And far beyond our world
countless suns rise and set
in the infinity of the universe,
before worlds never imagined
and misty globes scarcely fathomed.
Somehow, astonishingly,
always glorious
always spectacular
always stunning.

Part Three

Letters from Bali and India

Letters from Bali and India

*I*n *the summer of 2004, I traveled for the second time to Bali, Indonesia, and for the first time to India, where I freestyle backpacked and journeyed by bus and train throughout the northern part of the Indian country. The following letters and stories, chronicling this international adventure, were originally sent by email to a group of friends, family members, and colleagues. Also included are several, never-before shared, travel journal entries. The finale of my journey brought me back to the States via Hong Kong.*

The author, writing on the deck of the *warung*,
Bali, 2004. Photo by Dario Berrini.

Subject: Greetings from the Island of the Gods
Date: June 20

Bali is beautiful. The entire vibe of the island is deeply spiritual. The people are gentle, their traditions are a fascinating blend of Buddhism and Hinduism, and they are quite loving and devotional. The streets, even in the most remote areas, are often lined with statues and carvings of Buddhist and Hindu deities. Woven baskets filled with fresh, tropical flowers also line the streets. They are offered daily in reverence to the Gods and Goddesses.

The trip over here took a total of twenty-six hours. I spent the first three days visiting with my good friend, Randall Hayward, who now lives in Bali full-time and has co-founded Taksu healing spa and retreat center. Randall lives in the mountains, several hundred feet above the Ayung River in the lush, tropical heart of the island. It was great to reunite with him and also join my surfing buddy from San Diego, Dario Berrini, who has been traveling for several months now. During the first few days we got massages, ate like kings (curried vegetables and tempeh are a staple of Balinese cuisine), and stayed mostly in the highlands.

After that, Dario and I headed for a very remote part of the west coast of the island to surf and be close to Mother Ocean and her blue waters. The journey was about four to five hours by car to a tiny village called Balian. We are now living in a *warung*, it's a thatched-roof, bamboo tree hut. We actually climb a ladder to get up into it. The cost is equivalent to roughly $5.00 (U.S.) per night. It shakes and sways as the wind blows, and seems quite unstable at times, but it's not. Balinese villagers have been living in them for centuries. We do, however, meet lots of interesting bugs.

The *warung* has a large wooden deck where we keep our surfboards and practice yoga. From there we can smear our noses across plumeria flowers in the treetops and gaze at surrounding, glimmering green rice fields. The *warung* also provides us with a stunning view of the Balian surfing point which harbors a fantastic array of waves. The surf has been ranging from five to nine feet. It's quite powerful, but softened by the warm, eighty-degree ocean water.

I've had intense, lucid dreams since arriving here, many involving friends and family from home. The dreaming could be a result of the wet earthiness of this land, the amazing floral fragrances, and the elaborate carvings and sculptures of deities that seem to be everywhere. It's hard to say, reality here is so different and uncommon (by our standards), but certainly incredibly deep and inspiring.

Subject: Bali High
Date: June 24

The village of Balian and its marvelous stretch of coastline have provided me with life-long memories. The local villagers are sweet and humble, many are rice farmers and fishermen. Cows and chickens roam freely through lush, green hills, and people smile here—big WIDE smiles. Women and men wear traditional, colorful sarongs and often roam barefoot. A tiny street runs through the village to the sea. In the afternoons, women come and go balancing baskets of rice or fruit on their heads. This is a side of Bali that is still virtually untouched by Western ideologies. The Balian people are Hindu. In this "lost" part of Bali, though we lived close to the earth and more or less camped-out in our *warung*, we ate at least one meal each day at a local restaurant in either Balian or nearby Medewi. Local cuisine is based around locally grown rice, tempeh, vegetables, and fresh coconut-milk curries and peanut sauces. A huge vegetarian meal would cost us no more than a few dollars. Balian has left me with peaceful eyes, a relaxed smile, memories of long, peeling, turquoise waves, and a few jellyfish stings. Living in our tree hut has left me with more than seventy mosquito bites! (Yes, I counted. Balinese mosquito bites are quite intense—many of them turn into huge welts, so I've come to know each of them well.)

Fortunately, almost all of the bites are on my legs and feet, and between essential oils of tea tree and lavender, and several hours of soaking them in saltwater everyday via surfing, they have not bothered me too much. The strange thing is, these mosquitoes are so sly here I could never catch them biting me—and my organic citronella insect repellents have basically been useless. It's all good though. Ultimately, there's a give and take in every aspect of our lives. If you want to live in a *warung* on the tropical coast of Bali, there's a price. The same is true with our modern, everyday conveniences—our cars, our technologies, our fast-paced lives, our jobs… Everything has a price, an effect, a result, something that must be given or sacrificed. We have so many choices to make…

On the fourth day at Balian, I broke a fin on my surfboard during an amazing morning surf session. Fortunately, there were a few spare surfboards in the village. One was a classic, rainbow green, mid-1970s single-fin. Dario and I resurrected this board, which probably hadn't been ridden in decades, and after a few quick repairs it was ready for the water. The thing is—some Balinese villagers never wear or use the color green on or around the ocean. Green is reserved strictly for the Goddess of the South Sea, a mermaid-like deity known as Nyai Roro Kidul. There are numerous local legends about her power and her curses, and the Balinese villagers simply don't fool around with stuff like that. So here I am walking down the trail to the sea with this bright green, 70s single-fin, reluctantly daring the Goddess to notice me. An old Balinese fisherman approached, stopped me, looked at the board, and then said a whole bunch of things in Bahasa of which I understood nothing. I looked at him and smiled, looked down at the board, and then gestured with my hand toward the ocean. I wish I knew what he said, but he closed our encounter with a laugh and one of those sweet Balinese smiles. I felt it to be his way of warning me, yet offering me a blessing. My own ceremony to the Goddess of the South Sea (and every other Goddess I know of—just in case) followed on the hot, black sand before I entered the ocean. I then paddled out on that green piece of surfing history with total humility, a good dose of cautiousness, and a great respect for the powers that rule the surrounding land and sea. What happened? My session was marvelous. It was like going back in time to another era, and I felt rushes of that universal Goddess energy enfolding me on every wave. The session turned out to be one of the most highly-charged, spiritual surfing experiences I have ever had.

Overall, my time surfing and exploring the remote west coast of the island with Dario was phenomenal. Since then, I have been spent the last few days in the town of Ubud, and relaxing at Randall's house in the lush highlands. Ubud is considered to be the artistic and spiritual heart of the island, and is home to many of Bali's most adept wood carvers, weavers, and sculptors. As I mentioned in my last letter, Balinese art is a celebration of their deep spirituality, their sincere relationship to their Hindu faith, and the Hindu and Buddhist deities whom they honor. We saw the beautiful dance performances of Barong and Legong, where dancers in colorful, traditional Balinese costumes enact stories from the Hindu epic, Mahabharata. They were accompanied by a live *gamelan* (traditional Indonesian music) orchestra of about twenty-five villagers with various percussion, drums, bells, gongs, and flutes. Inspiring!

With a mixture of reluctance and excitement, later this afternoon I will depart from this glorious island paradise and begin a new journey as I head to India. In a handful of hours, I will fly to Hong Kong and catch a connecting flight that will bring me into Delhi, India around 1:00 a.m. tomorrow morning. After a couple of days of settling into India (if such a thing is possible), I plan on seeking out my Tibetan Buddhist monk contacts at a temple in Delhi and journeying to McLeod Ganj, a suburb of Dharamsala, in the extreme north of India. Another adventure begins...

The author, atop the *warung* after surfing the legendary
Green Goddess single-fin. Photo by Dario Berrini.

Subject: Delhi is Berserk!
Date: June 26

Just a note to keep myself connected to some sense of familiarity. I use this email travel journal as a way of reflecting on my experiences and sharing them, but also (especially now) to keep emotional contact. So thanks for being there.

Delhi is absolutely insane! There are approximately fourteen million people living in this massive city and most of them seem to be dwelling in extreme poverty. The streets are out of control—and I've seen some really heavy and intense places in all of my travels—but this place is beyond any of them. The goal here is simply to survive. Things are filthy. Living conditions in the heart of the city are horrendous. There's very little consciousness of health here. The focus for many seems to be on finding water to drink (even if it's dirty), food to eat, and avoiding being run over or stepped on. Even spirituality seems to hover on the far fringes of life. Death is lingering everywhere.

Of course there are exceptions... women roaming in their bright-colored saris, people hustling to work, government palaces and business centers, etc. But mostly, the streets are filled with cars, busses, soot, smog, grime, motorized scooters, trucks, auto rickshaws (basically three-wheeled, motorized golf carts), and bicycle rickshaws. People line the streets, some standing around, others walking, sitting, limping, meditating, sleeping, begging, dying... Traffic scurries like rats moving in every conceivable direction simultaneously. A guy on a scooter crashed into our auto rickshaw. Nobody was hurt. The two drivers yelled at each other for thirty seconds and then it was over. My rickshaw driver (who I spent about three hours with today racing around Delhi) soared the wrong way down one-way streets at approaching busses, and raced around like a teenager playing on the bumper cars at an amusement park. But he's not alone. That's the way they do it. This is the Delhi ride at Disneyland's new India theme park. Only it's for real and people are dying!

Drivers are constantly honking their horns, and just as often avoiding potentially dangerous accidents by inches. Animals are everywhere… skinny, wandering dogs… cows and bulls lying by the side of the road. At one point, as we raced through traffic, there was an elephant walking down the middle of the street. Scooters charged in front of her, rickshaws tailed her giant feet, honking. She roamed unfazed. These are no little country roads, but pothole-ridden, paved streets lined with broken-down shops and littered with trash. I saw a family of five on a single scooter. Dad drove, little boy was on his lap, two girls sat behind, one on mom's lap. I don't know how they all fit, but they were doing it. Zipping through madness! Teetering on the brink!

I've seen some extremely seedy parts of this city in the mere couple of days that I've been here. One could get swallowed up for good in this seething sea of humanity. It's hot, muggy, and there are people who appear to be wandering hungry in every corner. I don't feel comfortable eating here so I'm living off purified water, bottled juice, spirulina powder, and some energy bars and snacks that I brought with me.

Tomorrow my rickshaw driver will meet me and take me to his favorite Hindu temple, a Sikh temple, and some other special sites that he knows about. His name is Shog-Vedi. He is fifty-four years old and says he has a son about my age. I'm glad I found him—he patiently drove me all around the city searching for a safe place to stay. The conditions of some of the budget hotels are so frightening one would be better off wandering the streets or staying up all night. (I'm referring to small rooms with dirty concrete floors and rats or cockroaches scurrying about!) But I'm tucked away in a little room that's fairly decent. I've seen some Indian businessmen in and out of here, but I haven't seen one tourist. Not that I expect to, because I assume most Western tourists go to five-star hotels and stay away from most of the intensity and filth that Delhi is so full of. Maybe they're smart.

So after some temple visits tomorrow, Shog is taking me to the bus station and I'm outta here. I'm going north to Dharamsala by overnight bus that takes about fourteen hours. I plan on finding my way to McLeod Ganj, a

Tibetan Buddhist colony in the mountains loaded with temples and monasteries and stunning views of distant Himalayan peaks (so they say). It'll be nice to see a completely different part of India... and to continue on with my journey.

Toto, we're not in Bali anymore.
I'm survivin'—that's my goal!
Peace... from the edge of the world...

Travel Journal Entry
June 27 (evening)

Reflections from a brief journey through the ghettos of Delhi...

In the slums of Delhi
death lives on every street
hell abides in every hungry body, in every thirsty soul
anguish thrives in each churning stomach, in each shivering, feverish body
and envy flourishes like an invasive weed in the heart of each precious, desperate, poverty-stricken human being...

In this moment
I believe it is fair to say
I am fleeing hell by bus...

I am finally on the overnight bus to Dharamsala and miles away from Delhi. What utter chaos that place is, especially in comparison to the island paradise of Bali. It's almost unbelievable, the poverty is horrendous. Countless thousands of people are homeless, living in tents, lying in the street, drinking filthy water from the gutters... Meanwhile people relieve themselves anywhere and everywhere, and the smells alone are nauseating. It's absolutely disgusting. You can taste the suffering...

A one-armed young woman was desperately following me... begging... but she wanted more than food or money. She wanted *me*... my belongings, my clothes, my body. I felt as if she would devour me, consume me, or become me, if she could. Even one's soul is not safe in such an environment.

And the travel agents themselves, where I purchased my bus ticket just a few hours ago, were outright thieves. They overcharged me in every possible way... and they worked in tandem, one would distract me while the other would attempt to steal from me by digging in my backpack! It was purely insane.

I indeed feel like I am fleeing hell by bus. Glad to be away from there and on my way to new experiences, although I feel devastated for all the unfortunate people who cannot escape the suffering and the horrid prison of their own lives as rupee-less residents of the slums of Delhi…

Subject: Between the Extremes
Date: June 29

Thoughts from Dharamsala…

The extremes that I have experienced in India since leaving Bali have been simply mind-blowing, stretching me to the edges of my own heart and mind. My last day in Delhi was both interesting and challenging. At my request, my rickshaw driver, Shog (who I have come to really appreciate and trust), took me to see several of Delhi's most beautiful temples, including the largest Hindu temple in Delhi, a smaller Hindu temple dedicated to Lord Shiva, a Baha'i temple built in the shape of a lotus blossom, and a Sikh temple where I happened upon *bhajans* (devotional songs) performed by three bearded men in turbans playing harmoniums and *tablas* (Indian hand drums). I also visited Mahatma Gandhi's shrine where I felt what I can only describe as the sweetest, most loving vibe I experienced in all of Delhi. The serenity there helped carry me through the rough spots of the day and the remainder of my time in that most overwhelming city. I won't go into details now because they're quite gruesome, but if you read my last letter you can imagine what I mean. But let me just say, your imaginings can only scratch the surface of what is a common, terrifying reality for so many people over here…

The overnight bus ride from Delhi to Dharamsala proved to be one of the most insane bus rides of my life, and as such, offered its own set of challenges. Much of the road, especially through the mountains, is narrow and mauled with potholes. To compensate for this, bus and truck drivers tend to drive in the middle of the road—at night, and around blind curves. When an oncoming vehicle approaches, there's a dangerous game that plays out between the drivers. They continue at full speed in the middle of the road, as if preparing for head-on collision, and then moments before the crash they blow their horns as each vehicle swerves out of the way to avoid certain death. Why do they do this? I can't really say. I can only say that they do it—and it goes on all night long…

So after what turned out to be a grueling, fifteen-hour, all night bus ride, I arrived (virtually sleepless but happily alive) at the mountain village of McLeod Ganj in the Dharamsala region of Northern India. It's beautiful, peaceful, and clean up here... with giant mountains, pine forests, and Tibetan prayer flags waving in the wind...

McLeod Ganj is a small village with an international scene. There are shops filled with Tibetan handicrafts and garments, yoga classes, and cafes that claim to cook all of their food with sterilized water. Most of all, however, McLeod Ganj is home to Tibet's exiled spiritual leader, the Dalai Lama, and headquarters of the Tibetan Government in Exile. I am currently staying at the Namgyal Tibetan Buddhist Monastery in a quiet room surrounded by hundreds of monks, nuns, and Tibetan families who have fled their Chinese-occupied homeland for the safety and freedom of India. My room is simple, but it's all I need. My view faces the Dhauladhar Mountains and the Kangra Valley lying below. The monastery sits at an altitude of approximately six thousand feet, while surrounding peaks rise to elevations beyond twelve thousand feet.

I arrived at the village around 8:00 a.m. Monday morning and immediately headed for the Namgyal Monastery, hoping they would have an available room for me. There are several Buddhist monasteries up here, but Namgyal is the largest and the main one, seeing that it includes the Dalai Lama's personal residence. To my surprise, the paths that led through the narrow streets and up the hill into the monastery and temple grounds were crowded with people—Tibetans, Indians, even Westerners. Turns out the Dalai Lama was in town (he's often abroad or in the U.S.) and a special ceremony, which he was administering, had just begun. About an hour later, and after somehow gaining admittance into the most sacred region of Namgyal, I found myself sitting amidst hundreds of robed Buddhist monks, gazing into Tsuglagkhang and peering at the Dalai Lama seated cross-legged, with a big smile, on an elaborate throne of cushions.

Tsuglagkhang is Namgyal's main temple, a beautiful shrine where the most important ceremonies are held. It houses three absolutely stunning statues: the historical Buddha, Shakyamuni; the great bodhisattva of compassion, Avalokitesvara; and Padmasambhava.

These grand, immense Buddhist images rose boldly into the room, seeming to possess their own life and awareness. Tibetan horns blew and cymbals crashed while the Dalai Lama, along with several hundred other monks and Tibetans, chanted ceaselessly. The ceremony continued for about two hours, complete with drums, bells, and incense. It then climaxed with the Nechung Oracle (a great Tibetan spiritual prophet) dressed in elaborate, ceremonial costume, going into a deep trance and dancing in the middle of the temple. It was extraordinary!

After the oracle collapsed into what seemed an unconscious spiritual state of some kind, the Dalai Lama was escorted out, along with the oracle, by a small entourage consisting of senior monks and personal guards. For another two hours, however, hundreds of monks remained seated and continued to chant. I too remained... sitting quietly... wrapped in my purple Balinese sarong... smiling... and experiencing what I felt to be total absorption in the moment. Intermittently, Tibetan horns sounded and cymbals crashed, shattering the droning of the monks' voices. Surely, I had drifted off to a sweet, deep place I haven't been to in quite a while... or at least since Bali.

Enjoying the breaths, between the extremes...
More to come...
Namaste!

Images of Avalokitesvara (above left) and Shakyamuni Buddha (above right) from inside Tsuglagkhang. Om mani padme hum. Photos by the author.

Subject: From Dharamsala
Date: July 2

It is very peaceful up here in the Tibetan Buddhist land of Dharamsala, India. Every morning I am awakened around 7:00 a.m. by several hundred monks chanting in Tsuglagkhang, which I found out is also called the Dalai Lama's temple. From my room in the Namgyal Monastery, I can see the surrounding Dhauladhar Mountains, which are part of the Outer Himalayas. I usually spend a few minutes taking in the view and then join the monks for a few hours. The chanting is all in Sanskrit and it's quite elaborate, so I am not able to actively take part, but I sit with them nonetheless, meditating and soaking up the overall sense of peace. I am greeted with such kind and loving eyes from the Tibetan people. One day the chanting broke around noon for lunch (rice and vegetables—all vegetarian) which I was invited to share. After lunch, the monks held a karma-purification, fire ceremony in the temple courtyard. Senior monks chanted over a large fire burning specific herbs and sacred wood, while others, dressed in ceremonial attire, added to the chanting and the crackling of the fire with deep, rumbling blasts of Tibetan horns and crashing cymbals. It was very powerful and moving...

The Dalai Lama has been here and has been involved in some of the ceremonies, but he is said to be leaving any day now for Spain. His whereabouts are often kept secret for his own privacy and safety. I gave a copy of my newest book of poems, *Sea-Soaked Heart: Thoughts from the Pacific Coast*, to one of the Dalai Lama's personal aides to give to "His Holiness" (as he is called up here). I wrote him a note explaining who I was and that I was staying at the monastery. The aide assured me he would pass on my book to His Holiness as soon as possible. I get a kick out of thinking about the Dalai Lama reading Soul Rider ocean/surfing poems!

So what's it like up here? The village of McLeod Ganj is actually very busy right now. The narrow streets are filled with people and lined with shops selling mostly Tibetan handicrafts, assorted bronze buddhas, singing bowls, tapestries, etc. The shops seem to be about sixty percent Tibetan-owned and forty percent Indian-owned. There are plenty of restaurants and an assortment of internet cafes. Cows, mules, and dogs roam the cobblestone streets along with the people. The funny thing is, the animals up here don't "belong" to anyone. They just exist freely, wandering wherever they want, looking for food, sleeping where they choose—often in the middle of the road.

There are definitely people living in poverty here, but nothing comparable to the conditions in Delhi. However, things in the village are not clean, you must be careful where you go, what you eat, what you step in, etc. There are several thousand Tibetans (in addition to all the monks) living in McLeod Ganj, and although they live on very little and are quite poor by U.S. standards, they live well, with self-respect, humility, and happiness. Overall, the Tibetan people are clean, deeply spiritual, and very close-knit. They definitely have a solid sense of community and look out for one another. Tibetan-owned shops have signs reading, "We do not sell items made in China." Their Tibetan culture is strong and their Buddhist faith, philosophies, and practices are thriving. I would guess there must five or six hundred monks living in the monastery and a couple of thousand more living throughout the village. Overall, this place feels more like Tibet than India. I guess that's why it's known as "Little Lhasa." Hats off to India for providing sanctuary to the Tibetan people and their government. Nonetheless, it's clear that the Tibetans miss their homeland and their relatives who are still in Tibet, many of whom they haven't seen in years, even decades. The movement to "Free Tibet" is alive and well with many fresh, brilliant minds involved.

Westerners who come here tend to range in age from the upper-twenties to the mid-fifties and consist primarily of Europeans, Australians, and quite a number of Israelis who are escaping the tensions in Israel. Few Westerners come here to actually study Buddhism, most come just to get away from their own country or other parts of India. They tend to be a sincere and soulful group of travelers—most that I've met anyway. The majority of visitors to McLeod Ganj, however, are not Westerners but middle and upper class Indians on holiday.

Fortunately, the Namgyal Monastery is on the far southeast end of the village, up a hill, and is fairly secluded. Most tourists don't spend much time over here. I seem to be the only oddball standing out (although trying to keep a low profile) during the daily chanting services. I'm definitely the only foreigner staying at the monastery. Some of the monks have become quite curious about this sarong-wearing, scruffy-looking white dude hanging out in their temple courtyard all the time. Some that speak English ask me where I'm from, others that don't often flash me that sweet, compassionate Buddhist smile.

Usually I leave the monastery around 1:00 p.m., take a walk through the hills and watch the monkeys, and then spend the rest of the day roaming in the village, getting food, writing, etc. The road leading from the monastery down to the village can be intense. Often it's sprinkled with an assortment of Indian beggars, many of whom are either crippled in some way, missing portions of limbs, or have strange diseases where it looks like their fingers, toes, or even limbs are rotting away. They get your attention by calling out "Namaste!" as you walk by. I try to help some of the hungry every so often. There are a lot of people in serious need, and for roughly $4.00 (U.S.) I can buy a mother rice and milk that will last her and her children for two to three days. It's fascinating—the clashing of people up here... the Tibetan community and monks that are really close... the Western wanderers who look to live inexpensively... the wealthy Indian tourists that come here to shop, see the Buddhists, and relax with their families... the Indian shop owners who are somewhere in the middle (economically speaking)... and the poor Indian families who resort to daily begging in order to get food to eat. Lessons and opportunities are everywhere... we just have to keep our eyes and minds open...

All in all, I am thoroughly enjoying the Buddhist vibe up here and soaking up the peace as much as I can. Soon enough, I'll find myself moving on to other parts of India... perhaps to the yoga capital, Rishikesh... and after that maybe Varanasi, the holy city by the Ganges, which is said to be a total shock—outdoor cremations by the river, roaming sadhus, etc. We shall see...

Senior monks of the Namgyal Monastery. Photo by the author.

Subject: Beyond Cloud and Wind
Date: July 4

Mist hangs heavy over the highest peaks of the Dhauladhars,
shrouding them in secrecy.
Only on occasion are we treated to rare glimpses
of their craggy, snow-capped summits...
Wind blows cool through pine forests...
Where am I?
This is a land beyond time...
My eyes open now
as mist parts
burned away by afternoon sun...
Beyond lies even higher stretches of Himalaya...
home of Gods and Goddesses...
My eyes close again
and I'm carried by the monks' chanting
beyond my cross-legged form,
beyond space
and concept...
beyond cloud and wind...
where thoughts cease
where whirling energy finds stillness
where identity finds formlessness...
I am both lost and found
in the blasting of Tibetan horns
the pounding of drums
the crashing of cymbals...
I am both lost and found
in this ancient land
in the rich spirit of the Tibetan people
in the depth of their ancient traditions...

Here in Dharamsala, the monsoon rains have arrived. Downpours are heavy. The streets are mobbed with Indian tourists. The monks have been silent for two days now. I think they're creating the balance for the upcoming huge celebration in the temple courtyard for the birthday of His Holiness, the Dalai Lama, on June 6. He won't be there, but the entire local Tibetan community will.

A couple of nights back, I had a quiet, late night, full-moon walk through the village with a band of friendly, roaming dogs who guard the temple complex. Such sweet, intelligent animals… highly in-tune and aware.

Travel Journal Entry
July 5 (mid-day)

I've spent seven nights so far at the Dalai Lama's Namgyal Monastery. This morning, I was invited into the monastery's headquarters to have tea with Tenzin Dawa, the General Secretary at Namgyal. He's a very kind, older gentleman who is quite friendly and curious about Western visitors and America in general. We talked about life, culture, travel, spirituality, and of course, Buddhism. He suggested I take a day trip today to the Gyuto Monastery and meditate with the monks there. He also mentioned that the Norbulingka Tibetan Institute is a very special place nearby which holds some of the most treasured, sacred relics of Tibetan Buddhism, including historical writings and ancient Buddhist thangka paintings that were smuggled out of Tibet by escaping monks after the Chinese massacred thousands of Tibetan men, women, and children in 1959. After tea, Tenzin and I shook hands and he smiled at me with the most sincere eyes. I walked outside to the sound of Tibetan horns and watched the clouds part to reveal massive Himalayan peaks in the far-off distance. I stood on the balcony with one of the monks, taking in the view in silence. I was overcome with emotion. I could feel myself in the midst of profound, personal transformation. The beauty and overall depth of my experiences of the past week and beyond have been so deep and moving that as I came back into my room, I began to weep...

Buying shoes for a little boy in McLeod Ganj (pictured above left with his mother). The rhesus monkey (above right) is common in Northern India and abundant in the Dharamsala region. Although they can be very aggressive, pack outcasts from troops living in the hills of McLeod Ganj often found their way to the monastery grounds where they lived quite peacefully. Photos by the author.

Subject: The Whistle Blower
Date: July 6

The last few days have been truly fascinating. India continues to stretch my ideas of reality. I've had tea and shared meals with Buddhist monks curious about this Western visitor. We've had engaging conversations about the world, spirituality, and the affairs of nations. I visited the stunning Gyuto Monastery and Tantric University in the nearby mountains, home to the 17th Karmapa. There, I shared rice with senior monks and attended their afternoon puja (fire) ceremony. I also hiked to the base of a huge waterfall outside a small mountain village called Bhagsu Nag and baptized myself in the pure, high-altitude waters...

On the way back from the falls, I came upon a very old, semi-dilapidated Hindu Shiva temple frequented by a small group of local, rural Hindu villagers. Three sadhus (Indian holy men) with long dreadlocks run the place and live in an adjacent brick cave. I sat and meditated with these guys on the dirt floor of their house-cave for a while. Suddenly, somebody began ringing the temple bell and the sadhus joined in with gongs and drums. I grabbed a pair of large hand cymbals and we were off on a twenty-minute, instrumental, musical jam session followed by chanting. Again, this wasn't a neat, cozy temple with shiny instruments, but a dark cave with incense burning, a small fire cooking an old pot of rice, piles of ragged blankets lying around, and occasional scurrying mice! Yes, these sadhus live in a cave in virtual silence with very little food and almost no possessions. Date and time dissolve amidst this stuff...

The birthday celebration of the Dalai Lama was filled with traditional Tibetan and Indian music, dance, and festivities, and was something special to witness. It began with dawn chanting and went until 1:00 p.m. Interestingly, when I arrived here at the monastery, it was the day of the sacred ceremony honoring the memory and birthday of Padmasambhava—the eighth-century Indian Buddhist master who brought Buddhism to Tibet. And now I will depart—later this afternoon—on the birthday of His Holiness. I'm trying to grasp the meaning of this, but I think it's beyond my current understanding.

The hip hangout in McLeod Ganj is a place called Om Restaurant and Hotel. It sports a rooftop terrace with outdoor tables looking down thousands of feet into the Kangra Valley. It's also one of the more reliable restaurants in the village when it comes to clean and healthy food. It's owned by a Tibetan Buddhist family, the restaurant is all vegetarian, and they don't serve any alcohol. It's a cool place where Western travelers gather and swap stories about their journeys through India. It seems that most everyone has a Delhi story or two. Since getting to Dharamsala is quite a feat in itself, some of the stories are about nightmare bus rides like the one I shared previously. One of the most intense India travel stories I've heard so far is about a route into Dharamsala from another village in the north. This route involves travel through one of the highest drivable roads in the world. Apparently, the road is so poor and narrow that many busses have driven off the edge, tumbling thousands of feet into the mountainous gorge below.

Some travelers reported that on this particular nightmare bus ride, the bus company (and these are usually fairly run-down busses) perched an Indian man on the roof of the bus with a whistle. Every time the wheels of the bus got so close to the edge of the road that the bus was in danger of falling into the ravine, the man blew the whistle, notifying the driver that they were all about to die if he didn't turn inward. (No guardrails around here, folks.) People on the bus were terrified and nearly had heart attacks every time the man blew the whistle, which was quite often! It's no surprise that travelers usually only do this route one way. If they make it, they choose alternate routes, or jeep travel rather than bus, for their return.

How's this for a bit of info: The Tibetan waitresses who work in the Om Restaurant earn the equivalent of six cents per hour!

So what's my plan? I'm leaving shortly by local bus to begin a journey through the mountains to a town called Pathankot. From there, I'll get an overnight train to Rishikesh. I don't know if my bus will have a whistle blower or not. Hopefully, I've soaked up enough of this sweet Buddhist peace to carry me through the next phase of my travels. It's hard to leave here… the peace of the mountains… the serenity of the monks… but other parts of India call.

Images of Shakyamuni Buddha from the Norbulingka Tibetan Institute's *Seat of Happiness Temple* in Sidhpur, Dharamsala. This marvelous gilded copper statue is approximately fourteen feet tall, one of the largest of its kind outside Tibet, and is considered a rare, sacred masterpiece. Photos by the author.

The young monks of the Gyuto Monastery (above). Tibetans celebrating the birthday of His Holiness, the Dalai Lama, on the grounds of Namgyal (below). Photos by the author.

Travel Journal Entry
July 6 (late night)

Sitting here on a bench outside a seedy, rundown train station in Pathankot... waiting for my overnight train to Rishikesh. It's after 11:00 p.m. and it's so hot and humid I can hardly stand it. I thought I was going to get mugged on the walk over here from the bus station. It was a long walk through dark streets with peculiar characters hanging out in pitch-black alleyways. It seems like this town only has limited electricity because everything is dark—homes, shops, streets. Either that or there's some sort of city-wide power outage right now. I'm not sure what's going on, but it feels very economically depressed around here. Strange...

The bus ride from McLeod Ganj was nothing short of insane! The old, semi-broken down, piece of shit bus was packed with probably 120 people. Three people per seat! People coughing, groaning, moaning... children and babies crying. Armpits in my face! The woman sitting next to me was begging from me half the time... wanting me to feed her, give her money, etc. I had nowhere to go, nowhere to escape to, and she just kept looking at me with sad eyes. She seemed so unhealthy and poverty-stricken, but then so did many of the people aboard the bus. I've never been in such a closed-off space with so many people who seem sick or diseased. It was extremely challenging. It definitely pushed me beyond the edge of my comfort zone, for sure. The guy sitting behind me kept coughing on the back of my head! He was coughing so close to me that the wind from his cough was blowing my hair. This went on for hours. I tried to ask him to stop, or at least put his hand over his mouth, but he did not seem to understand me. And the whistle blower! I can't believe I experienced the whistle blower. It was so intense! A few times I really thought we were going to slip over the edge and tumble into the ravine thousands of feet below. It was truly terrifying! Death seemed very close this afternoon. I had to continually practice surrendering and letting go. Home seems so far away right now... wherever home is...

The infamous bus. Note the large roof rack. Up there, amidst the luggage, is where the whistle blower sits. Photo by the author.

Travel Journal Entry
July 7 (early morning)

What an absolutely brutal, grueling night! I believe this is the worst travel experience of my life—I'm referring to this freakin' train ride from hell! It's about 6:30 a.m. and the so-called sleeping quarters in this train car is mobbed with people smoking, coughing, and lying around everywhere. It's hot, sticky, and smelly. The stale air is filled with cigarette smoke and the scents of dirty, sweaty feet and horrendous body odor. It's awful. Conditions are SICK! I forgot to mention the stench of urine. People just pee in the corners of the train! There's not even a bathroom—just a hole in the floor where you squat over and release everything onto the speeding tracks below. Beggars board the train whenever it stops and ask for money. Obviously, I barely even slept… it feels more like a jail cell than a sleeping car. What a horrible train ride… and I've got five more hours to go—at least!

Additional note: It seems like eighty percent of Indian men smoke cigarettes… and when people cough they have absolutely no concept of covering their mouths. It's almost unbelievable. I've never seen such filth and disease in all of my travels—and I've been to some wild places. It's moments like this when I wonder why I ever left the pristinity of Bali. Damn, I had it made… surfing beautiful waves and eating pure, healthy food in an island paradise. Amazing how quickly reality can shift. Hanging by threads on the way to Rishikesh…

Subject: Through the Streets of Rishikesh
Date: July 9

Monsoon rains
pour from dark, misty skies
washing litter, urine, phlegm, and cow dung
through dirty streets trodden with Ganges-soaked Indian pilgrims,
primarily males between the ages of fifteen and forty.
They come on spiritual holiday
to wash themselves clean in India's sacred Ganga River...
its brown waters rush along unconcerned...

Watch your step!
Piles of rain-soaked cow dung
steam
in the ninety degree heat and outrageous humidity.
One cannot help but breathe in the stench...

Sadhus wander
dreadlocked, bearded, and nearly naked,
wrapped in dirty orange shawls...
one wears a human skull hanging from his neck.
Beggars approach with open hands, mauled hands, missing hands...
Cripples limp... babies cry...
Packs of visiting Indian youth march through the streets
shouting "BUM BUM" in honor of Shiva
as they make their way to the river... brown, wide, sweeping river...

Shops welcome western visitors:
YOGA, MEDITATION, MASSAGE...
Used bookstores beckon
with racks filled with spiritual books

on every imaginable type of yoga
by every imaginable yogi:
Ramakrishna, Ramana Maharshi, Paramahansa Yogananda,
Swami Rama, Vivekananda, Sri Mata Amritanandamayi, Babaji…

A British traveler said:
"India is a rollercoaster,
about all you can do is hang on and try to enjoy the ride."
One American had the time of her life
studying yoga for five weeks in Varanasi…
One Brit was mugged there…
One Israeli was knocked off her scooter and had her backpack stolen…
Some had marvelous experiences with local people…
Others ended up on IV's in Delhi due to terrible food poisoning…

You can't control India
you can't fight it
eventually you just succumb to it…
or—if you're capable—relax into it
and almost become it.

One does not travel through India
rather India travels through you.
Its very essence surrounds and enfolds you…
You breathe India
you wear India
you sweat India
you cough India
you defecate India
and if you're really unlucky—
you even vomit India.
(So far I haven't been that unlucky.)

This is India...
in all of its wretched glory...
This is India...
in all of its lovely insanity.
All in all,
it's one of the most mind-blowing
and ENCHANTING
lands I have ever visited...

Subject: Update from Rishikesh
Date: July 10

I've been in Rishikesh for three and a half days now. The journey here was very challenging and took more than twenty hours. The bus ride down from Dharamsala was unbelievable... Three people per seat... Armpits in my face... Listening to the whistle blower...

Yes, my bus had a whistle blower perched atop the roof amidst our luggage and bags, and indeed he blew the whistle many times. The most frightening moment was when we had to pass another bus that was traveling up the same narrow mountain road as we were heading down. The road, at that point, didn't appear to be wide enough to accommodate both busses safely, but neither bus driver was willing to yield or back up, so we just remained there, facing one another with engines idling—and occasionally revving—as if engaged in some suicidal game of chicken. Finally, after ten minutes with neither driver willing to compromise, both busses began to drive toward each other. The drivers were careful, but as we approached slowly it became obvious that a clear passage was impossible. Still the busses crept toward each other, scraping sides as we slid past, the whistle blower atop our bus blowing madly as our rear wheels were almost hanging off the edge of a thousand-foot cliff. I could almost feel the sensation of beginning to slip off and tumble into the ravine. While some passengers were terrified, others seemed nonchalant about the whole situation, as if it were normal or commonplace and there was nothing at all to worry about. The scraping of busses continued until finally both rear bumpers locked and nearly tore each other off. With a final thud, the bumpers gave way—presumably dented and twisted out of shape—and we were free and on our way to continue our descent down the mountain. There's more to the story, including my window-seat perspective of the busses scraping together and the terror in the eyes and faces of passengers on the opposing bus. However, I'll leave it at this for now. The rest shall be a story for another time... perhaps in person upon my return...

In some ways, even worse than the bus ride, was the thirteen-hour, over-night train ride packed with people sweating, smoking, spitting, and snoring, and my attempts to rest amidst the smells of dirty feet and urine! It felt more like a moving prison cell than a train.

As for Rishikesh, it does indeed have its own unique and special charm. There are ceremonies in the mornings and evenings by the banks of the Ganges. Devotees float candle offerings down the river to the singing of *bhajans*. It's quite beautiful to experience. I've done some yoga, and have been studying *sitar* and *tablas* with a master teacher. However, with Indian tourists and monsoon heat and rain, it's just NOT the time to be here, so I'm leaving by night train to Varanasi—said to be one of the most wild, insane, and holy places in all of India. Here comes another train ride… eighteen hours!

India, O India…
You are indeed a land swirling with contrasts…
Serenity, filth, spirituality, hunger…
Bliss, suffering, prayer, grief…
India, O India…

View of Rishikesh along the banks of the Ganges River (above), and
Lord Shiva (below). Om Namah Shivaya. Photos by the author.

Travel Journal Entry
July 10 (9:15 p.m.)

I finally made it to the Haridwar Railway Station where I'll take an over-night train to Varanasi. What an adventure getting here! First, a seemingly endless walk with my pack and gear through Rishikesh. Then, a completely berserk, one-hour taxi ride in heavy traffic with horns constantly honking. The streets were filled with crowds of marching Indian youth, hollering and chanting in their orange-colored clothing. As if that wasn't enough, the taxi could not get me all the way to the train station due to the traffic and blocked streets, so the driver had to let me out. I then found a bicycle rick-shaw to get me the rest of the way to the train station, but even that was an ordeal. Hours and hours of travel just to get here, and my train journey has not even begun yet. What a trip this country is! And what a sight this train station is! I can't even describe it... the lobby is filled with people lying on the floor! Just a pile of bodies! Some are sleeping, some are eating, some look sick, some look like they're dying right here on the train station floor. I've never seen anything like the scene in here...

Bodies sprawling, Haridwar Railway Station. Photo by the author.

Subject: Om Namo Shivay
Date: July 13

Update from Varanasi...

If it could be said that I was looking for something in India, a certain experience, or perhaps another particular piece of the grand, universal, spiritual puzzle (besides my experiences with the monks in Dharamsala and the whole Tibetan Buddhist thing), I seem to have actually found it in this ancient, holy city by the Ganga (Ganges) known as Varanasi. The awestruck quality apparent in my previous letters is gone, and I have a strange peace about me as I roam the banks of the Ganga with a peculiar comfort and a distant feeling of familiarity. In short, Varanasi is one of the most amazing places I have ever seen.

Believed to be the chosen residence of Lord Shiva, Varanasi is one of India's (and the world's) oldest and holiest cities. Just making it here is a great blessing according to Hindus, but to die here, be cremated, and have your ashes tossed in the Ganga, assures one of *moksha*—or liberation from the cycle of death and rebirth. Hindus come here to live, but more specifically, to die. Some of the dying wait out their last days in hospices near the city's main *ghat* (a series of steps leading down to the water). Others die in the street or beside the river.

The whole city and its 1.6 million residents are stretched out along the Ganga, with various *ghats* (which bring to mind grand stone steps leading to ancient Roman temples) every block or so, allowing easy access to the river. Each neighborhood actually has its own *ghat*. The locals use the river for daily bathing, washing of clothes and dishes, and even for relieving themselves. All sewers lead to the Ganga, boats fish from it, and children play in it, jumping and diving off the high steps into deeper parts of the river. The Ganga, in greenish-brown hue, glides along very slowly throughout Varanasi.

Although there are so many potentially mind-blowing forces operating simultaneously in Varanasi, there is an extremely deep spirituality here, a holiness, a peace, almost an ominous peace at times, that permeates everything along the banks of the Ganga. The feeling here, the ancient quality of the city, the sacredness of it, is a little like the feeling I've experienced in the heart of Old Jerusalem in Israel, but without the religious tensions. The old city and the buildings along the Ganga have an architectural majesty like that of Rome; while the relaxed feeling of the slow-moving, placid river, the gliding boats migrating up and back carrying visitors to various *ghats*, brings an elegance like that of Venice, Italy. Add to this an intense, elusive, spicy flavor that only India can offer, and you have a hint—only a hint—of what is Varanasi.

There is a very sacred holiness here, all along the Ganga. People are praying constantly. Devotional music, singing, and *bhajans* can be heard everywhere... all over town.

Cremations take place in two distinct areas, at two particular *ghats*. One can see bonfire-like funeral pyres burning... dark smoke rising... local workers chopping and preparing wood... and dead bodies wrapped in shawls constantly being whisked to the banks of the river by family members. The bodies are "cleaned" in the Ganga, and then burned over piles of wood for three hours. Ashes are then dumped into the river. Holy persons, sadhus, pregnant women, children, and certain others are not cremated, but rather their bodies are sunk in the Ganga, or simply tossed into it to float away...

When ashes are dumped into the river, they are done so in huge amounts due to all the wood that is burned with each body. The river, along the banks of the cremation *ghats*, is often black from ash, and local pilferers enter into the dark waters to dig in the ash and mud in search of gold—jewelry, earrings, even teeth—from those recently cremated.

Down river, at the next *ghat*, people bathe unconcerned as to what was dumped in upstream... and further down river, people visit the banks for their toilet... and yet further down river, people gather water to drink, and children swim and play... Nobody is concerned.

Varanasi, as you'd guess, has its own unique smell. It's partly the smell of the river, as it's constantly evaporating from the 104-degree weather and its essence fills the humid air. But in spite of what one would think the smell to be with all the outdoor cremations going on, there's actually a very sweet fragrance beside the Ganga. I believe it's the result of the wood used during the cremations, as well as the massive amount of incense that's burned daily throughout the city. Everybody and everything seems to smell the same. Stated another way, the smell is a musky wetness, a sticky, sweet, smoky, honey-wood herb smell... the smell of the Ganga. It's not a foul smell at all, just a different smell, like nothing I've ever experienced... an intriguing smell, like the oddest variety of rare temple incense. Amazingly, there are not too many bugs here either, besides flies.

I am living in a place called Hotel Temple on the Ganges run by a very sincere, devoted, and friendly group of Hindu men. I pay less than $5.00 (U.S.) per night for a simple room, and they cook me awesome vegetarian meals for about $1.50. The rooftop and balconies provide amazing views of the Ganga and the meanderings of locals on the south end of town. The day begins at 6:00 a.m. around here (even for me), and by 11:00 a.m. I feel as though I've already lived a full day. I roam the river banks, moseying about the various *ghats*, shirtless, with my Shiva beads around my neck, soaking it all up... taking it all in. I've even managed to get some of the local sadhus to become quite curious about me. Imagine that!

This is the final leg of my journey. Bali seems almost like a lifetime ago. From here, I will eventually return to Delhi and then depart for the States via a stop in Hong Kong.

Images of Varanasi, the holy city on the banks of
the Ganges. Photos by the author.

These young boys spent hours each day finding recreation along the
Ganga. No skateboard or surfboard, but still they found a way to get air.
Airborne, upside down, in mid-flip (above). Just climbing to the top of
this seemingly abandoned domed building (below) was a task in itself.
Hurling yourself off and into the river below took some genuine courage.
Teenage thrill-seekers creating their own X game. Photos by the author.

At times, the ancient, dilapidated architecture of Varanasi reminded me of the post-apocalyptic world that was the setting for the original *Planet of the Apes* films that premiered in 1968.

The collection and preparation of wood for the numerous outdoor cremations is a constant process. The keepers of the fires are worthy of great respect, having to labor amidst intense heat, humidity, and the potent smoke of burning bodies (above).

Varanasi, along the banks of the Ganga... where dog and
goat rest together as friends. Photo by the author.

Subject: Culture Clash
Date: July 24

I am currently in Los Angeles, having recently returned from my journey to Bali and Northern India. I'm feeling well, although still readjusting to the time change. I have thoroughly been enjoying the many blessings of our culture and the California lifestyle—fresh organic foods, clean water, family, friends, and the beautiful Pacific coast and its shimmering blue waves.

My flight back to the West Coast from Delhi landed me in Hong Kong for a day. I was stunned by the spotlessness of the city. The high-tech airport provided multiple computer stations in every terminal with free internet access. The bathrooms were so pristine one could eat from the floors and drink from the sinks. (I almost did.) Everything seemed so different than India. I took a high-speed train into the heart of the city and was awestruck by the modern architecture and massive skyscrapers, as well as the lack of litter and the lush, volcanic landscape. Yet at the same time, I could feel the tightness of the culture, the expectations to stay in line, to know your role, and to look, dress, and act "appropriately."

Somewhere between India and Hong Kong there's a balance. Is the United States this balance? Perhaps, but not necessarily. Social constructs and thus lifestyles can be just as varied here in the U.S. depending on factors such as one's location, economic status, religion, personal beliefs, familial values, and regional social expectations. One could argue that there are aspects of both India and Hong Kong here in the U.S. But what we do have, additionally, to a certain degree anyway, is the opportunity to choose how we want to live. That's the blessing. Some of us live Hong Kong, some of us live Delhi... some decide to work hard and dress nice, others choose to play hard and live in a more relaxed manner... some practice law, others practice yoga... some fix cars, some sell real estate, some dance, some teach, some surf, some raise families, others sleep beneath freeway overpasses... some design clothing, others design software, some plant trees, others chop them down... The

American comes in virtually every size, shape, color, and style imaginable. That's amazing.

On the other hand, Americans often seem tense in comparison to Indians, and especially in comparison to the Balinese. I can't help to notice the extreme traffic in Southern California, and the tension and frustration that grip people. We're easily angered and waste no time in expressing it. Even worse, we can be arrogant or ungrateful to the point that we feel justified to be angry or frustrated when things don't go our way.

A sadhu in Varanasi said to me with a big smile upon finding out that I was an American, "Oh yes, Americans, you love to fight!" He didn't say it with criticism or condemnation, but more with a celebratory tone, as if to honor the premier quality with which he associated the American culture and its people. In the face of this friendly, yet over-generalized accusation or characterization of Americans as being people who "love to fight," I could only respond, "Not all of us."

But on a cultural or global scale, the classification posed by this blissful Hindu holy man was quite accurate. In examining the politics of our nation, the streets of our cities, and the tension on our roadways, it is reasonable to conclude we are a "short fuse" culture, often lacking in patience and tolerance. Thus, truly, lacking in wisdom. We have much to learn from the spiritually-focused, smiling sadhus in India who, by our standards, have nothing. We have much to learn from the patience of the Buddhist monks, whose practice it is to be present and at peace with the eternal moment, the ever-present NOW, in all of its flawed perfection. We have much to learn from the hungry, who seek not wealth, new cars, success, or popularity, but to be fed. We have much to learn from the children, especially those in India, who in spite of poverty, hunger, and disease, climb the high steps beside the main *ghat* of the Ganga and with huge smiles take three running steps to the edge and jump off, cannonballing into the dirty river twenty feet below. Joy, happiness, peace, compassion, can be felt, experienced, offered, and shared just about anywhere, anytime, with anyone, in the face of any condition, however extreme, if we choose it to be so.

There's obviously much more to be said about all of this, but I'll stop here with my sweeping homecoming reflections for now. Thanks for allowing me to share my journey with you. This email travel journal saved me a number of times from completely losing contact with Western reality and abandoning my life and identity in India. Just think, if it weren't for each of you, perhaps I would be wandering the streets of Varanasi right now, meandering along the banks of the sacred Ganga… shirtless and bearded… chanting and singing… lost forever (or perhaps found)… with the sadhus.

On the balcony of the Namgyal Monastery with the Dhauladhar Mountains behind. The Himalayas, shrouded in clouds, are barely perceptible in the background. Photo courtesy of one of the monks.

Part Four

Between Two Worlds

Between Two Worlds: Of Man and Deer

I moved from Encinitas, California to Wilmington, North Carolina in September 2002 and lived in the South until January 2008. During that time, I worked as an elementary school teacher. Specifically, I was an English language specialist and worked primarily with young, Spanish-speaking children who had recently arrived from Mexico and other Latin American countries. As a lifelong Californian, it was an interesting time in my life, marked by tremendous change in both geography and culture. The South presented me with daily opportunities to reexamine my views of the world and become tolerant to both religious and social viewpoints that, at times, I perceived or judged to be narrow-minded, prejudiced, or even downright igno-rant. In hindsight, although having traveled to many foreign lands, the mainstream culture of the South and its Bible Belt ideologies, challenged me more than many remote, international locales. Perhaps it can be argued that there are not too many places on the planet as foreign to the California surfer as the American South. The following is a true story.

It was a dark November evening as I drove the wooded, coastal North Carolina road home. My mind wandered and I flashed on a deer. Occasionally I see them skirting the woods by the side of the road or romping in the foliage as I pass by in my truck. I've always been a lover of deer and other animals, and years ago while visiting ancient Buddhist temples in Nara, Japan, I was privileged to visit Deer Park, an area where tame deer roam freely, having peacefully coexisted with Buddhist monks for centuries. They're beautiful and wise creatures with a majestic gentleness scarcely seen in humans.

Unfortunately, neither Deer Park nor Buddhist monks reflect the gen-eral picture of modern civilization. Certainly this is not the state of affairs in most of the Western world. Thus, like many of the other byproducts of our civilization, as I drove home this particular evening I presented a noisy disturbance to the peaceful world of the deer and offered them nothing but possible danger. Together with my truck I'm blinding headlights, roaring engine, and steel beast that could take the life out of them in an instant. To the deer, I suppose most humans are seen as executioners of a sort. A theory that is only deemed more credible when taking into consideration the sad fact that there are those of us whose hobby it is to dress up in camouflage and kill deer and other animals for sport.

This particular night when I flashed on the deer however, I didn't actually see one, but imagined one. As my mind continued to drift with the dark curves of the road, I dreamed. I wondered what it would be like to hit a deer—how terrifying, traumatic, and sad it would be. I thought of what it would be like to slam on my brakes and run out into the cold night to check on the animal as it lay on the lifeless pavement. As my thoughts continued, I found the beautiful creature still alive, though gravely injured. I panicked, wondering what I could do at this hour to save it. In a desperate flurry, I grabbed a plastic tarp and a towel from my truck, wrapped the deer inside it, and lifted it into the back of my truck. I thought about the blood spilling out, and hoped it would not be too much of a mess. Could I save it, I wondered. Which room will I bring it to? The garage? The enclosed patio? It's going to freeze tonight, I've got to keep it warm. I imagined myself tending to its wounds, giving it water, and trying to nurse it back to health.

These thoughts flashed before me not through long contemplations but in brief instants. This vision, this encounter with this deer, happened much like a dream, in mere seconds, as I passed a certain stretch of road on the way home. Like a dream that the mind experiences during two or three seconds of sleep in which countless details can be extracted and recounted, and rich events experienced, such was this vision. It all passed before my mind in twenty or thirty seconds, and then before I knew it I slowed down and pulled into the driveway of my house.

The rest of the night was like any other night, although I flashed on the deer scenario on several occasions. Soon enough, however, it was time for sleep and my eyes closed for the night.

The morning came quickly, and I found myself driving on the same stretch of road in the opposite direction on my way to work. I was running a little bit late, and since it was daylight I increased my speed on the narrow, wooded road. Suddenly I spotted something on the side of the road ahead of me. My thoughts of the deer from last night, lost somewhere in my subconscious mind, gushed forth into my waking reality as I passed by a large animal lying dead on the roadside.

No, it can't be, I whispered. Was that a deer? Damn. Surprised, saddened, shocked, I wondered how this related to my vision from the previous night. Before these thoughts had finished passing before me, I had sped by the animal. I found myself braking and trying to look in my mirrors to verify that it was, in fact, a deer. Before I could find a place to turn around, several cars had crept up behind me. The morning commute was well under way, and even in this more rural part of Wilmington, North Carolina, rush hour traffic was a definite concern.

I've got to turn around, I thought, but they're all on my ass! I exhaled loudly. An opposing voice within surfaced: You're already late for work, dude. If you turn back to look at that deer, that animal—whatever it is— you're going to end up even later and have to explain to the principal why you felt the need to stop for an already dead animal on the roadside.

Doesn't sound so good, I thought. Well, I can make up another story, I pondered. Still momentarily struggling with whether or not to turn around, and where to do so, the decision was at last made for me when I reached a local elementary school. Unfortunately, it was not the school that I worked at, that one was across town. This neighborhood school represented a point in my morning commute where traffic from four different directions bottlenecked with school busses and parents delivering their children. It seems as if nobody walks anywhere anymore, myself included.

It was too late to turn back now. I had missed my chance. Going back at this point was unfeasible. It's okay, I thought, I'll look for it when I come home this evening.

For the rest of my drive to work, the experience dominated my thoughts. Maybe it wasn't even a deer, I entertained, and there's nothing meaningful about any of this. Maybe it's all just coincidence. Why do I always have to find some connection in everything, I questioned. Maybe there's nothing mystical about any of this, nothing transcendent of our humdrum, materialistic, superficial sense of reality and mundane existence. Maybe I'm just trying to grasp for a more natural, connected lifestyle during an age where such connections have all but been severed. This event, or non-event perhaps, may only symbolize my disconnectedness from the life I truly should be living, or want to live. Which is? Well, I pondered in this mock conversation I was having with myself, which is more simple, more in touch with nature, more in touch with my own nature and my relationship to life, to the natural world, to the powers of nature, to God... but not God as in old man with beard, rather God as in unexplainable, transcendent power and love, perhaps, that unites all things in a very real, yet completely mind-boggling and mystical way. Yes.

So maybe the lesson, I offered myself, is in trusting and honoring that side of myself. I don't have to *know* that the animal was a deer, I can *feel* that it was, and perhaps understand that there was some connection with that animal and myself the previous night, before it was hit, while it still roamed the earth. Maybe I was sensitive enough to pick up on something, to feel it before it happened, as animals can sense storms approaching.

I remember as a boy back in Los Angeles leaving the gate open and our dog, Scruffy, escaping. He was gone for several days, and yet, shortly before—or after—an earthquake, he came running home. It could have been chance that he just happened home on or about the time of a rather significant Southern California earthquake. But I knew then, or I guess felt, that was not the case. He was gone, he was cruising, he was exploring, and then he sensed this terrifying event, this earthquake, about to happen, and he raced home as quickly as he could. He was scared for himself, for us, yet he was concerned for us, his family; he wanted to help, to be there, in his own dog way.

Okay, so either I have an active imagination or I am simply open to things that somewhere along the recent lines of our developing civilization, perhaps the period of industrialization, we have forgotten, we have lost. This loss being our very conscious connection to life on this planet and our place in the universe.

Soon enough I reached work and all those thoughts about mystical connections to life, and accepting that it was or was not a deer on the road that morning, had to be pushed aside. There was work to do, children to teach.

Later in the day, around lunchtime, I began chitchatting with one of the two school secretaries, Sue Barnhill (yes, that really is her last name). She was a cheerful, heavy-set, happy-go-lucky woman in her upper thirties, and was rather open-minded and easy to talk to. She was fun, and tended to keep things going at the school in her own friendly, graceful way. Yet, if I'm not mistaken, Wilmington, North Carolina had been her home for her entire life. Actually, the school at which I was teaching, the one she worked at, was the same school she attended growing up. Nonetheless, probably due to the fact that I wanted additional human input, I shared with her details of my encounter with the deer the previous night, and what I saw on the road that morning. She was interested, even curious, and she entertained the idea that maybe I actually foresaw something before it happened. Hmm.

Surprised and somewhat pleased to find an interested party, I began opening up more. I brought up one of my favorite books, *The Man Who Killed the Deer* by Frank Waters. Waters was a noted twentieth-century Native American anthropologist and author who specialized in Pueblo Indian culture and history. This particular book, perhaps his most renowned work, portrays a young man growing up in the Pueblo nation sometime in the mid-late 1800s. The young man, Martiniano, had been taken from his village at a young age, as many children were, and placed in a government mandated "white" school. The school was designed to strip Pueblo children of their culture, customs, and heritage and teach them the ways of the encroaching white world. However, when Martiniano finishes school, there is no place for him in white society, nor does he desire one. Thus he returns to the pueblo, only to discover that he is shunned, perceived as a sort of traitor, one who has forsaken his Indian nature and adopted the white ways.

True, there were things about him that were now different. Some of his Indian ways had been lost; rather they had been stolen from him, forcefully stripped away. In the white schools they were beaten for speaking their tribal languages. But he had not become one of "them" he told the people of his pueblo. Nonetheless, they had seen many good Indians converted. In fact, a number of their own people who too had been taken from the pueblo and placed in the white schools now worked for the very government agencies that dominated Indian affairs. Further, many of these converted Indians headed government committees intent upon restricting Indian rights and freedoms. The government felt it beneficial to approach Indians with Indians when it came to political matters, or matters of restricting their rights or available land usage. Thus it was with due cause that the people and elders of the pueblo had grave concerns with one such as Martiniano returning to the pueblo after all those years of white education.

In Waters' story, the pueblo council votes to allow Martiniano to stay, but he is made to live outside the limits of the village, on a nearby hill. He opts out of traditional ceremonial dances, refuses to take part in normal religious procedures, and even experiments with a peyote cult in his quest to find belonging; yet he still maintains his own personal identity as a Pueblo Indian. Martiniano eventually marries outside the pueblo and begins to raise a family in a small, self-built shack on this infertile, barren hillside overlooking the pueblo and his people.

As the story progresses, Martiniano, in need of food for his family, goes hunting. He ends up killing a deer, as is customary. The deer will help feed his family for the ensuing winter; its hide will be used to keep his pregnant wife warm. Unaware of new tribal laws imposed upon the pueblo by government oversight committees, there is now a deer-hunting season. Martiniano, mistakenly, though at the same time rather unconcerned, has killed a deer outside the scope of this allowable period and now he must be prosecuted, punished, by both the tribe as well as the white world. What ensues from this point forward is an incredible story about two clashing cultures with completely different ways of viewing reality, of living on planet Earth, and of a young man caught between these two opposing worlds. It is also the story of the decline of a marvelous way of life and the loss that the world has suffered at the hands of modern Western society.

But there is more, the deer. The deer that Martiniano has killed serves as a powerful spiritual force in the story. The spirit of the deer becomes a sort of haunting overseer, a natural force that brings deep-seated concerns and issues out of hiding to be examined, to be dealt with. The deer that Martiniano has killed is part of a real, natural consciousness that links all the life on this planet together as one; and ultimately and eventually this holistic, all encompassing life consciousness demands a certain balance of living and non-living forces on the planet...

Sue Barnhill was looking at me with wide eyes, and had rather speechlessly nodded on occasion as I summarized the story and recent happenings with passion and fervor.

"Sounds interesting," she chimed at last.

It was around that time when the other secretary of our school, Connie, offered her two cents. Connie was quite a bit older, in her sixties. "Old enough to be your mother," she had informed me on several occasions, usually it was while she was instructing me on some matter of school policy of which I was unaware. But she was nice, loved to chitchat, enjoyed gambling as her favorite hobby, and sneaked away every couple of months for a few days of rolling the dice in Atlantic City. She too had spent the majority of her life in Wilmington, North Carolina. After all, she had been the secretary here when Sue had been a student. (Do any of these folks ever leave?) Connie was divorced, had one adopted son—a high school senior, and the highlight of her year was usually her annual trip to Mecca—or rather, Las Vegas.

While Sue was more of a classy Southern belle, Connie was tough and at times harsh. She was a smoker and drinker with a rough voice, a woman who had probably grown up in the country around a slew of redneck, Civil War Southern boys. Though Sue and Connie were very different in both age and character, they worked together quite well. Certainly, neither of these women could be pushed around and they knew how to hold their ground with the best of 'em. Ultimately, they ran an excellent elementary school.

Connie hadn't heard the whole story, but she had heard about my desire to rescue the deer, take it home and nurse it back to health. She had also caught bits and pieces of my synopsis of Waters' book. She thought of me rather fondly as a sort of California beach boy, a charming outsider unaware of the way things must be done in the real world, the South. But Wilmington, North Carolina was changing and quickly becoming a kind of cultural hub; a place where northeasterners were escaping to for warmth and affordability, a place where Latinos were coming for economic opportunities, a place where even California surfers like myself were coming to sample the waters of the Atlantic. Nonetheless, at that time I was still a novelty in the South, an original, the real McCoy, if you will, and was crowned with the nickname "Cali" upon my arrival and shortly thereafter dubbed "Malibu" by a young waitress after chatting with her for a few minutes.

"See ya, Malibu," she had sung from across the restaurant as I departed.

But then there was Connie, with her own captivating, motherly, redneck charm.

"Mah son wantsa learn to surf. Maybe you kain teech 'im."

"Sure Connie, anytime," I'd respond.

So Connie had heard enough of Cali, of Malibu, talking nonsense about rescuing a deer and all of this other California gibberish, and it was time she set the record straight.

"Let me tell you somethang, you kaint put a deer in your car," she bellowed. "You hit a deer, you leave it, hear me? That thang'll kill you. There was a woman, just recently, who did that very thang. She hit a deer, stopped, it was still alive so she tried to play he-ro and rescue it. Well, let me tell you, that thang woke up in her car and trampled her alive."

"Wow," I interjected.

"This here's the absolute truth," she continued, "that woman is dead!" She paused, nodding her head, affirming what she herself had said.

"I had no idea," I mumbled, unsure of how to respond. "I didn't actually do this," I stuttered, "I mean, I only thought about doing this."

"You just leave them thangs alone if you hit 'em. You see," she continued, "they get stunned... the headlights, gettin' hit... everythang. But then they wake up a few minutes later, and I mean it, them thangs'll trample you alive. This woman was crushed in her car. Them damn thangs are dangerous." She concluded her lecture with another nod and then, to my surprise, a long, exaggerated inhalation through her nostrils nearly identical to that quirky trait performed by Don Knotts' famous character, Barney Fife, from *The Andy Griffith Show* (which incidentally was set in a small town in North Carolina). She closed our encounter with a snicker and walked away. That was it, she was done.

Unbelievable, I thought to myself, that's all this woman has to say about my story. It wasn't until later, and after some reflection, when I finally conceded that perhaps what she was offering me was actually good advice, maybe even crucial Southern wisdom that someday might really come in handy. Hmm.

But for the time being, at least for the rest of the school day, I decided I would just keep my mouth shut. I mean here I am this California surfer, a spiritually-minded naturalist of a sort... into yoga and Eastern philosophy, having just returned from an awesome trip to Peru... rethinking my life, my path, my purpose... and in the process of realizing that the modern, materialistically-driven, Western world and I don't mesh... yet I am living in the Bible Belt of the United States. Most people don't think about saving deer out here, they think about killing deer.

As the day continued, my thoughts flashed occasionally on the deer, and though I wondered what the connection was, I decided to let it go for the time being and look for the animal on my way home from work. I was also okay with the possibility that I may never understand the situation, or find out if the animal on the road was even a deer, and may have to surrender the whole scenario, or accept it, as one of life's elusive mysteries.

On the way home that afternoon, I looked for the animal but did not see it. I assumed it had been removed, or perhaps tossed into the adjacent woods by those who lived nearby. Later that evening, a couple of hours after sun-down, I left my house to meet some friends for dinner. It was another dark night, and as I approached the spot where I had seen the animal, I slowed and carefully eyed the side of the road.

My God, I exclaimed, there it is. I pulled over ten feet from the carcass, leaving my engine running and the lights shining on the now lifeless creature. Sure enough, it was a deer, a beautiful female, not quite fully-grown. I stood there in amazement, pondering my connection to this creature, wondering if there was some understanding between us, some relationship between us during the last moments of its life. I wondered if perhaps my conscious mind had just barely scratched the tip of the possible remarkable connections among the sentient beings of this planet. And yet I couldn't help to feel that this deer was another casualty of our civilization, another unnec-essary death, or at least a death at the hands of our culture.

While in Peru, earlier that month, I had been wandering through a little shop in Lima, communicating with the store owner in my broken Spanish, when an elderly man approached.

"De que pais?" he asked me. What country are you from?

"*Estados Unidos*," I responded.

"Oh," he countered, shaking his head, and then went on to tell me that as an American I had messy hands covered with blood. From Iraq and Afghanistan to various exploitations around the globe, America had the blood of the world on its hands, he informed me.

I explained to him that not all Americans are aggressive or violent, and that many of us do not support or approve of the policies and procedures of our government, especially when it comes to military actions. Nonetheless, the old man shook his head in a disapproving manner before he departed.

What would the thoughts of the deer be? What would say the universal consciousness of life, this mystical spirit of the deer that Waters so powerfully alludes to in his story about Martiniano? One thing was certain, someone had hit this animal and had left it either dead, or to die alone on the cold roadside. The same treatment toward a human would be taboo, a crime that would land the perpetrator in jail.

So I stood there, by the cold, dark roadside, by the deer, illuminated by the lights of my truck, and I drifted again into that dream state. I pondered my own place in this odd world we've created. Cars drove by; they slowed and looked at me, perhaps wondering whom the idiot was in the Peruvian mountain hat, standing over the dead animal. But this deer means something to me. This event has meaning. And though I could see the curious looks from passersby, I mourned for the loss of life, for the loss of the deer, for the loss of our own connectedness to life. On this dark, cold evening I carried the weight of sorrow, and realized that I, like the young man who returned to his pueblo, am also caught between two worlds, the new and the old, the materialistic and the spiritual naturalistic. I am Martiniano, and this deer, however indirectly, is the deer that I have killed.

I am the outcast, the lonely wanderer searching for connectedness in an age of disconnection. I too am caught between two worlds, the modern and the ancient, walking and breathing that fine line of loneliness and fulfillment, of isolation and unity, of ignorance and wisdom, of sadness and joy. And though I rejoice in the beauty of the natural world, I mourn its loss.

As the cold wind blew across my face, and the lights of my truck and passing cars illuminated the earth around us, for a moment I understood my place and saw the path before me... between two worlds.

Author's Note: Frank Waters (1902-1995) was an American writer with Cheyenne ancestry, born and raised in Colorado. Along with The Man Who Killed the Deer *(1942), he also authored the renowned* Book of the Hopi *(1963) and many other novels and historical works related to the American Southwest and Pueblo Indian life and culture. The Frank Waters Foundation was established in 1993.*

The author at Nara Deer Park, Japan, 1997. Photo by Randall Hayward.

Part Five

The Vanishing Sky

Sacred Dust

There's a mysterious something
that falls from the sky
and drifts through the air
like a heavenly dust...
I've glimpsed it,
on the most beautiful of days...
like an invisible pollen
that lifts into the breeze from the most fragrant and colorful blossoms...
like the fresh blue mist that wafts from the tops of cresting waves
when the Santa Ana winds blow.
I've seen rainbows in that mist
and felt the brush of pelican wings upon me.

She too possesses this sacred dust.

There's a crescent moon in the sky tonight,
hovering...
I could hang the lasso of my love around it
and gaze back in wonder at this delicate Earth...

There are those rare beings
for whom we would jump off the edge of the world...
those rare, beautiful beings
who steep us in inspiration,
saturating us with something long forgotten...
We should hurl ourselves into them
as an unpolished stone into a vast sea...
diving into the abyss of oblivion, if need be,
to know and taste the truth that is there.
It's not about death

but reemergence,
for the sacred dust creates new life
just as the fragrant pollens stimulate new growth.

Only by tossing ourselves into this whirling, bejeweled mystery,
this fusion of earth and sky,
of fire and celestial mist,
of liquid and bone,
can we know the truth of our hearts.

Sometimes I think there are no answers here...
only more questions...
and this story has already been written.

She arrived with the moonlight
and first lit up a quiet unknown valley
in a remote land from my purest imagination...
Blue eyes gazing wildly,
captivated with the beauty that she is.
Now her pollen circulates me,
floating around me, around my bed,
like a miniature universe.
Beauty itself falls from her.
Like a child from a fairy tale
she leaves a trail of this invisible, sacred dust
wherever she moves,
though only the keenest eyes can see it
and the most open hearts can detect it.

I've inhaled it...
inhaled her...
and she courses through me...
through bloodstream, heart, and opened mind,
through lungs and sacred passageways within...

I feel her sacred dust, this divine pollen,
in the tightness that builds before the shedding of tears...
the shedding of needs...
the shedding of desire...
the shedding of identity.

Nay, I tell you, we don't know who we are yet.
None of us.
But something within tells me that this magic she has,
this beauty she is—
is who I am also.
So I inhale and exhale, move and feel,
in stunning awe,
in stunning awe.

--2013

Perspective from a Winter Ocean

There are no words…
only the hiss of white foam
and the distant roar of thundering surf.

There are no words…
only the hollow howl of wind in my ears
and the silent ringing in my head.

There are no words…
only the cold running through my body
and the heaviness of fear in my chest.

There are no words…
yea, scarcely are there even thoughts,
but raw, uncompromised perceptions.
For out here, amidst the cold fullness of this terrific sea—
immense, heavy, deep, dark—
and the tall, green swells,
there is only myself…
and life.

Author's Note: This poem is dedicated to the legendary Hawaiian surfer and waterman, Mark Foo (1958-1994). It came to me on a cold winter day while surfing a very large swell at a renowned San Diego surf spot called South Garbage. The verses seemed to spontaneously immerge while I was sitting far outside, between sets, waiting for waves. I can still vividly recall the fear and sense of isolation that I experienced this particular day. There was indeed an ominous energy in the ocean. The following day, during this very same swell in late December 1994, Mark Foo drowned while surfing Maverick's in Half Moon Bay, Northern California.

The Ends of the Earth (Continued)

To the ends of the earth we have come,
across the hundred million year-old landscape.
The indifferent, cold sea glares at us
as it pounds the falling cliffs.
Coyotes cry their lonely calls
into the grand, immense darkness
while galaxies spin through the vast heavens above.
Winds blow—
harsh winds,
cold and ceaseless.
Am I no more than a single speck in a mountain of dust?

--Punta Canoas, Baja California, Mexico, 1996

Land of the Maya

The silent power
the power of the wind
penetrates deep
through my skin
to my bones
through my bones
to my soul
where it stirs up
latent memories…

--Mayan temple ruins, Tulum, Mexico

The Frog People

I don't know anything anymore…
but did I ever know anything—
anything of value
anything of truth
or only that which was fed to me by the institutions of this culture?
Today I roamed with a good friend
amidst the desert-like chaparral of the Malibu mountains.
We crawled on hands and knees under bushes and brush
following a dried-out creek bed up to a series of rock formations
nestled at the base of a tremendous golden-red mountain peak.
The crunching of leaves beneath our feet signaled our clumsiness…
Two modern man-apes feebly trying to be silent
as we climb a once time-worn but now forgotten trail,
trespassing upon *private* land to reach an ancient Chumash site.
Hidden caves adorned with paintings
of strange amphibious human-like beings
remind us of our current isolation—
isolation from nature
isolation from land
isolation from earth
isolation from the medicine and fragrance
that the chaparral and sages possess
isolation from the pure, fresh air
isolation from wildlife
isolation from *wild life*
isolation from imagination
isolation from our own hearts…
Modern anthropologists refer to these human-amphibian beings

that the Chumash painted so long ago
as *frog people.*
Did the *frog people* symbolize the Chumash' connection with the water
their reliance on the nearby Pacific Ocean
their deep knowledge of the coastal creeks and saltwater lagoons
or did the *frog people* represent something more than mere symbolism—
something deeper and more profound that the humans of today
simply cannot understand and have no conceptual framework for?
Were the *frog people* real beings—
beings from the water
beings from another realm
transcendent mermaid-like beings
that were capable of breathing underwater?
We do not know.
We cannot know.
Later that afternoon
I pry a dead jackrabbit off the pavement of a mountain road
where it lay head crushed in a pool of its own blood
smashed by an automobile roaring through the Malibu canyons.
"Back to the earth, my friend," I whisper.
I don't know anything anymore…

Author's Note: Special thanks to my old friend and fellow adventurer, Soren Mitchell, for guiding us to this sacred Chumash site on this particular day.

Chumash rock art, *Frog People*, Santa Monica Mountains, Malibu, California. Photo by the author.

Cuzco

In my dream I traveled to a golden city
far below the sea
in the middle of the Pacific.
Glorious beings
greeted me with bright eyes
and heavenly love.
Know they the secrets of forever
but closed is their land to humankind
until rise we do out of our darkness.

The Refusal

The cold vapor of inhumanity—
that very substance which fills our cities
generates our wars
flows through our governmental facilities
spawns our greed
our thievery
and is the basis of mankind's global spirit of competition
rather than cooperation—
encircled me like an icy wind.
It gushed through me
forcing its slick fingers through my skin and into my bones
permeating me with its terror,
which is the madness of our world.
Reaching my delicate core
this shameful destroyer of human-beingness
stripped my vulnerable, vital essence,
creating wounds of isolation.

I s o l a t i o n

The wounds are the source of our separation…
our separation from source
from truth
from meaning
from belonging…

The icy vapor continued its destruction within me,
sucking out my very nature
and spilling it across the spoiled earth,
removing from me the last vestiges of my inner harmony,

creating from the once wholeness of my being
an empty vacuum
whereupon depth becomes shallow
meaning becomes worthless
and all understanding is lost...
truth becomes illusion
and illusion truth,
thus experiences cannot be trusted
but discounted as mere variations of pleasure and pain
of joy and sorrow...
This world that I perceive around me
although seen by my eyes
heard by my ears
inhaled and tasted by my mouth and breath
touched and felt by my very hands
and made animated by my own actions—
is unreality.
This false shadow
in which I live, move, and have my being and consciousness
is indeed mere fiendish illusion.

Illusion

Materialism is our religion.
Greed our most prized virtue,
and we have so skewed loyalty
as to make ourselves slaves to this self-inflicted confusion.

Hiding from truth
hiding from reality
hiding in darkness from the ultimate lightness of our beings
we stumble onward
believing that we know
believing that we are.

Deceived by the very illusions that we have created
to cope with our own sufferings we suffer more.
Onward we trudge,
deeper into falsity,
into a frantic unreality that can only create more suffering...
we stroll ignorantly
mindlessly
inhumanly
with no desire to look deeper...

Disoriented and satiated with televised commerciality,
lost in a hectic world of brainwashed superficiality,
we wander...
the peons of the universe that we have so devolved into...
ashamed, afraid of the ultimate marvelousness of our true natures.
Thus we throw depth to scorn
and refuse the search for awareness.

The Vanishing Sky and a Table for Two

The evening sky
brilliant with the shades of twilight
glows behind her
though she can't see it…
Beyond us,
to the west
the coastal clouds turn deep orange and fiery pink,
ablaze with the afterglow of sunset.

Her hand brushes lightly through her long hair and she looks up at me.
The surrounding twilight vanishes
before the beaming of her ocean-colored eyes.
My God, I've seen these eyes before!
Where?
I'm lost for a moment.
Distant dreams, memories perhaps, of faraway lands and ancient times
waft through me with the waving of her hair as she speaks.
I recall a surf session from many winters ago…

It was a giant northwesterly swell, so big that few surfers attempted it. Dolphins were swimming on the outside of our Leucadia reef and streaking through massive, shimmering blue walls of water. I remember being caught inside when a huge set closed out the beach. "Slow your breathing, stay calm, drop your heart rate," I told myself as I drew my last breath, tossed my board aside, and swam deep to escape the thunderous impact of this terrifying wave. It was one of the first of what became several near-death experiences for me in the ocean. But it's not due to the sense of drowning that I recall this episode now, here, over dinner. It's because of what happened in the mid-state, the point between life and death, between wakefulness and unconsciousness. For it was right there, under the water, in the depths of the ocean, when all my breath was gone, when all colors had faded, during that precious last instant of consciousness before passing out, when she appeared.

Sure, I'd heard all the stories—myths—about mermaids and Neptune's underwater world, but this was different. A dream? Perhaps. A vision? Maybe. But it stayed with me. She stayed with me, for quite some time, in both waking and dream-states.

She lifts her cup, takes a sip of water, and smiles.
Damn, who *is* this woman?
Is she of the ocean?
Does she even know who she is?
Do any of us really know who we are?

I glance at her hands, noticing the unique texture and color of her skin,
then shake my head in awe imperceptibly.
She is radiating something both alluring and intangible...
Neither of us understand.

The sky behind her has now grown even deeper in shade.
My gaze drifts momentarily beyond table and restaurant,
beyond shopping center, traffic light, boulevard,
beyond the streets filled with hopes, dreams, and struggles...
beyond treetops...
where purple-hued clouds blow in sea winds
and drift across the dark blue of encroaching night.

A single passing cloud draws me in...
We are that passing cloud,
that brief waft of wind that blows away the final glow of dusk...
And this moment, this encounter,
the gleaming of her turquoise eyes
and the backdrop of the heat lamp's fire upon the flaming red of her hair...
is a mere twinkle

in this most beautiful and brief
vanishing sky.

--Encinitas, California, 2013

Last Night a Dagger Struck Me

Last night a dagger struck me
it hurled off from somewhere within you
some mysterious realm that you not only inhabit
but that inhabits you
some incomprehensible, transcendent place
within your chest
where worlds are born
where stars collide
where a magnificent beat
and a profound calling
beckon me like a powerful, ancient song that I cannot resist nor deny

Last night a dagger struck me
it burst forth invisibly
propelled by the pulsations of your heart
and cut me open
deep
wide
spilling over me the liquid red of fresh love

Last night a dagger struck me
it twinkled and shimmered as it spun toward me
carrying the beaming blue of your radiant eyes
at once destroying and birthing me in your beauty
and now I feel you
and see you
everywhere
everywhere

On the Foot Bridge

On the foot bridge
floating above the ravine
surrendered to the flow of movement
amidst radiant sun and wafting breeze...
Branches interwoven
old growth falling away
fresh growth emerging...
Present, open, eager
in the midst of transformation
reinvention
death and reemergence...
Here
together
deep within the practice of patience and trust
alive
in heart
with love...

--2014

New Growth

Die
a little every day
let your old growth drop aside
let the brown branches fall away.
Make room for your new growth
your bright tomorrows.
Let young green leaves
and a new generation of tender chutes
rise up from the brownness of your yesterdays.
Die
fall away
that you may live again
fresher, freer, and more youthful and wise
than ever before...

Woman in field with flower, Santa Cruz Mountains,
California. Photo by the author.

Presence

i feel you
still with me today
body pressing against mine
i feel you
on my lips
in my breath.

sometimes
when we stop everything
and just gaze
at each other
so deeply
i feel myself
inside you
looking out through your eyes
breathing through your breath.

in these rare, sweet moments
the separation between you and i
between her and him
dissolves
and i wonder
which one of *us* or *we*
am i?

--2013

Fleeting Faces

Fleeting faces
cast to the wind…
Fleeting faces
cast to the wind…
Fleeting faces
once part of us…
Fleeting faces
now cast in dust.

The light behind the shadow
is the consciousness behind my mind.
The light behind the shadow
is the truth we all must find.

And there is always light
there is always light
behind every shadow
there is always light.

Fleeting faces
cast to the wind…
Fleeting faces
cast to the wind…
Fleeting faces
once part of us…
Fleeting faces
now cast in dust.

Now I know
who I really am.
Now I understand
who I really am.
Free free free
I surrender to Thee.
Now I know
who I really am.
Not me but I.
Not we but One.*
Now I know
who I really am.

--Planet Earth, Solar System of our Sun, Milky Way Galaxy

Author's Note: * *"You and I are not we but one," is a statement by the great Indian/Persian spiritual master, teacher, mystic, and Avatar of the twentieth century, Meher Baba (1894-1969), who was known as the God Man.*

Last Trace

As the last trace of the shimmering Pacific—
my dear homeland waters upon this ever so indefinable planet—
fades from my view
and only the bending of a mountainous horizon remains,
I feel the pangs of longing in my stomach.
The airliner climbs higher on its eastward journey
and the young woman sitting next to me
clutches the hand of her boyfriend beside her.
As I write this they snuggle together,
she happily and he with a far too casual air of aloofness.
Her dark hair falls smoothly around her face as she leans upon his shoulder.
On occasion she presses her arm against mine.

The airliner continues to rocket east
away from the setting sun and into the darkness of night
and my nose begins to tickle with sadness.
I wonder where I am returning to…
definitely not home
definitely not to that special person in my life.

It's rather unfortunate…
My connection to the Pacific is so strong
the surfing has been phenomenal—even spiritual
and I have many great people in my life out there
from friends to family
yet here I am heading back to North Carolina and the Atlantic coast
to occupy a four bedroom house alone.

He reaches over and kisses her with a cool indifference,
a phony slickness he learned from a Hollywood film.
The whole scene seems so fake.
Through the airplane window I can see only darkness.

The last trace of the Pacific is so far gone now...
so far gone...
and only strangeness remains.

--2004

A Bird's-Eye View of Twilight

A single, solitary seagull
glides high across the coastal sky
toward the incoming twilight.
Its flight… seamless, silent, smooth.
Trace bands of solar light
hover at the distant horizon
above that ancient, ever-mysterious ocean.
Feathery wisps of orange and pink cloud fade
and vanish slowly at the hands of the approaching night.

The gull soars.

I know that bird.
I know its flight.
I feel its flight…
the coolness of the air
the strength and agility in my wings
the sense of lift in my feathers
my beak cutting through the crisp wind
the familiar feeling of aloneness
the stark sense of presentness
the unknowingness of what this incoming night will bring
or where I will sleep.

We think we know who we are.
We think we know where we are.
But what do we truly know?
What separates us from the gull
from the fading sunlight
from the ocean

from the streaks of cloud that will soon vanish?
And what of that mystifying view from above
the curious world of humanity below
the scurrying of people
the endless parade of cars, of traffic upon highway?
Each vehicle piloted by another like myself
with a world of thoughts
of fears, of dreams, of desires...

The seagull sees it all.

Headlights and streetlights illuminate as darkness encroaches.
The salt-filled west winds lift the gull even higher.
Beak forward
wings wide
feathers spread
it darts across the coastal sky
continuing its journey into twilight...
into infinity.

Darkness is falling
night arriving...
We filter into our homes...
lights, electricity, television, warm meals
family, laughter, conversation...
Not for the gull...
always the rawness of weather
the wildness of nature
the momentary challenge of survival
the profound silence of a life without words
the depth of a solitary journey on a floating, spinning orb...

Fade and vanish, O twilight, O knowingness
into the vast darkness of mystery,

for we now come with wings spread
and minds free from thoughts and words...
only the swiftness of our streamlined flight
and the silence of pure awareness.

Part Six

Reflections from Peru

From the Misty Realm of Machu Picchu

"This place will change your life," whispered my good friend, Jorge Tuma, a humble, spiritually-driven Mexican man of forty-seven years who looked more like a youth of twenty-five. "When I first came here," he continued, "I was in my twenties. I've made it a point to return once every ten years." Jorge, now a bilingual translator for the court system in Long Beach, California, left Mexico City in his early twenties and began to travel the world in search of truth and personal meaning. His quest led him all over South America and then around the world. He journeyed throughout many of the world's premier sacred and religious sites, and even lived on a kibbutz in Israel for six months. All the while he sought a deeper sense of his own spirituality and firsthand knowledge of God. Somewhat ironically perhaps, it was during the beginning of his journey upon visiting Machu Picchu in the heart of ancient Inca Peru, where he found a power perhaps incomparable to anywhere else on earth. Now he has returned again, and on this occasion led a small number of us outside the archaeological zone, beyond the ancient temples and houses of Machu Picchu—which astoundingly model the configuration of the Pleiades constellation and are perfectly aligned for the June solstice sunrise.

Our goal was to climb Huayna Picchu, the large green mountain that looms in the distance above the ancient, legendary city of the Incas. It was a misty day, a rainy day, in this lush, tropical region of the Andes Mountains. The trail was steep and narrow, and before departing Jorge and I shared a small bag of coca leaves. We sucked and chewed on them as we trekked through the ruins of Machu Picchu to the pathway that would lead us to the top of foreboding Huayna Picchu. The native Andean people have used the coca leaves in their raw, unadulterated form for centuries. The sustaining power of the leaf is incomparable to any other pure substance, allowing Andean workers and farmers to perform rigorous duties at some of the highest altitudes in the world on minimal amounts of food and water. Unlike cocaine, of which a minimal amount is produced in part by an enormous amount of coca leaf extract, the pure coca leaf is non-addicting and has beneficial physiological properties.

Several hours later, upon reaching Huayna Picchu's summit at an elevation of nearly nine thousand feet, we were wet from mist and rain, out of breath, and a bit shaky from the rapid climb and high altitude. We took refuge on a series of giant boulders and passed around water, bits of energy bars, and more coca leaves.

Looking off the abyss, swirling masses of cloud rose and raced by us, mimicking the flight of gigantic, mythical birds. On occasion, the mist parted and revealed the stunning ruins below, Machu Picchu in its entirety, and the lush surroundings of mountain and river.

Throughout my time in Peru, I came to know the Andes as a sort of home, a place where I connected with a marvelous source of life, energy, and inspiration. It's a land rich in spirituality and history, and it reactivated an ancient part of myself which transcends time, culture, age, and religion.

While in Peru, I strolled the cobblestone streets of Cuzco, wandered the caramel-colored, Andean hills of the ancient Incan ceremonial site of Sacsayhuaman, meandered through the indigenous village of Ollantaytambo, and breathed the freshness of the Sacred Valley of the Incas. All the while, I came to understand that a great depth of human wisdom abides within these humble descendants of the Incas, whose Quechuan tongues spin words like silk across an ancient land that is nothing less than their very souls materialized into living earth.

Though my journey was far from over, I knew that this visit to Machu Picchu was to be a sort of apex; and not in spite of, but because of the added elements of mist, rain, and strangeness, this mysterious hike was somehow a life-changing point. My good friend, Jorge, based on both how well he knew me and his own personal experience, knew this to be true without a shred of doubt.

As we prepared for our descent from the rainforested rooftop of Huayna Picchu down into the village below, I heard a snicker. I turned to Jorge and caught the last flash of the glimmer in his eye and the slant of his smile. Behind him swirled the rising mist and cloud, perhaps representing our ethereal connection to the heavens. The rocks of the summit at our feet were the pinpoint of our consciousness and knowledge. Below us lay the world, our fears and struggles, and the lives upon which we would descend into once again. I paused for final reflection, breathed deep of the surroundings, flashed again on Jorge, and took my first step down the trail.

"That's it," he said softly, "now your life is going to change forever."

Basking in the spiritual power of Machu Picchu with Huayna
Picchu in the background, Courtney Acamo experiences
the bliss of Inca Peru. Photo by Mike Barnes.

Desde la Zona del Cóndor
(From the Zone of the Condor)

High in the Andean mountains I sit upon an ancient rock wall,
ruins that are part of the Incan Temple of the Sun at Ollantaytambo.
Traditional music of the Andes rises from the village far below
and wafts in the breeze...
bamboo flutes and wooden pan pipes,
their shivering melodies,
soar high into the zone of the condor,
the great Incan bird that symbolizes the heavens
and the people's living connection to the Gods.

I sit alone,
above the Sacred Valley of the Incas
yet watch the wanderings of the people far below in the village,
they themselves so much a part of the very earth that surrounds them.
The fertile valley stretches green and bountiful below me.

A Peruvian woman—a resident of the valley below—
who has been climbing the trail
approaches me with her young son.
Clad in colorful, hand-woven garb
with dark, weathered skin,
she smiles.
I offer a few words in Spanish
but she understands and speaks only Quechua.
Our eyes and smiles nonetheless communicate warmth and peace.

They pass...
and I am again alone
with the thin air...

the humming of the music from the village below...
the thumping of my heart...
the quivering of my breath...

Images from Ollantaytambo, located at an altitude of over 9000 feet. Peruvian women (below) prepare for a traditional agricultural ceremony. Top photo by Jim Cowing, bottom photo by the author.

Part Seven

Thoughts on Death

A Lesson on Death

Fear not death
for it is the destination of life—
a doorway to veiled mysteries which lay before us.
Fear not death
but hold it in awe
and respect it for its own life.
Face it bravely
and do not waste your thoughts worrying or dwelling.
Keep your spirit strong and awake at all times
so that you are ready.

When I die
do not grieve for my motionless body,
but pray.
Praise the energy of all life.
Praise the birds, the insects, the flowers, the trees,
and all else.
Praise life with your love and respect
for all things under the sun.
For I will be praying with you.

I may be part of a fresh field of wild grass,
or newly bloomed flowers stretching up toward the sun.
I may be a tiny hummingbird flirting with a spring blossom.
Or perhaps I will be a fresh, green seedling
sprouting from a moist forest floor,
growing rapidly with the gift of life
into the form of a marvelous pine—
towering with dignity and wisdom.
Perhaps I will be a fly inside your home,

trying to survive
only to be considered annoying and filthy...
or a beam of sunlight cast down upon you
giving you warmth and love.
Or I may be the crow, sleek and black,
mischievously cawing and circling above you.
Or perhaps I may be the new cells flourishing in your body.
Or I may simply be a dry, crusty weed
curling up under a scorching desert sun.

So do not grieve death.
The spirit of life is eternal and cannot be destroyed.
What we call death is merely a change of form—
and the spirit of life is forever changing.
This cannot be resisted.
So look upon death as a gain, not a loss.
Praise this change as you would praise all life and birth.
And remember... the night sky and its stars
are every bit as beautiful as the morning sun.

--1991

With My Dying Grandfather...
Ten Stories Above Los Angeles

These observations, perspectives, and reflections were scribbled upon several sheets of paper on February 16, 2002, while I gazed out of my grandfather's tenth-floor apartment window, a remarkable view from Westwood Village, Los Angeles. He slept right nearby, grappling with the intense discomfort of metastasized prostate cancer. Though he emerged from this sleep and regained himself temporarily, the illness ultimately led to his death three months later to the day.

High above the green tops of swaying palms...
their waving fronds swimming through the stream of air
blown afresh from the nearby Pacific...
High above the streetlights and traffic signals
adorned with resting pigeons surveying the street below...
High above the meandering pedestrians, the rush of traffic,
the blasts of automobile horns and whistling sirens...
Eye-level with the heavy sky, its film of overcast wintery gray
blowing over Los Angeles like a cool smoke...
Eye-level with the misty shroud of steadily approaching dusk,
where daggers of light descend through thin breaks in the dense cloud,
reminding us of the hidden sun,
the light that thrives above the world,
beyond the atmospheric hindrance of gloomy gray...
Here we are.
Here we gaze from the silence of your room
observing the scene below
the comings and goings, the livings and dyings of man.

From our vantage point, the blowing breezes of nature's ever-changing patterns and climates greet hustling people. Leaves shimmer and dance, clouds float past, while people roam about largely oblivious to all but what their limited awareness perceives.

Grandfather, I remember walking the boulevard with you and watching the world go by... Remember?

In the distance, acres of trees collide with tall office buildings, and the 405 and 10 freeways flow with that never-ending stream of passing cars, each operated by a soul, with a life, with dreams, pains, sufferings...

Yes, high above it all, beyond it all, we abide. My grandfather and I somehow momentarily separate from it, yet ultimately and always enmeshed in it, for I know in minutes or hours I will again descend into the world to wander about and make my way back home, to find my soul, fumbling again amidst the mass confusion, searching for meaning, for momentary glimpses of expanded awareness, for flashes of insight and transcendence...

Yes now, here, beside my grandfather I abide beyond the world, not within it, as the presence of impending death has reminded me of the fleeting nature of everything we believe to be real. Something mysterious and sacred is upon us. I sense the immutability of the soul. There is more to our existence than this ever-changing world.

Thus here I abide in such interesting and curious momentary transcendence, gazing upon the scene of life from this window on the tenth floor, and although I am somewhat physically and emotionally detached from what is below, I am somehow gloriously connected to it all in an intangible spiritual manner.

Yes, here I abide, sheltered in silence beside my dying grandfather who sleeps now, at last, peacefully. His body submitting to its final demise, his soul throwing off the heaviness of flesh, of bone, of ninety years of matter, gravity, and struggle, soon to fly again weightlessly with the shifting clouds and soaring winds.

The gray sky continues to darken into night. The city and streets below come alive with light. Once sleeping skyscrapers are reborn as office lights illuminate. A helicopter roars over Westwood Village. Far off, where the southern and eastern horizons blend into sky, a sea of city lights twinkle and shine. With each moment of ensuing darkness, more lights begin to glow... shimmering golds, distant twinkling pinks, glimmering whites and reds. Close by, apartment complexes come to life, movie theatres and restaurants shine invitingly.

We have walked those streets together, Grandfather, and sat in those very restaurants, chatting and laughing.

Traffic signals now blaze through the darkness, while the freeways, the arteries of the city, still flow with the ceaseless pulse of human life. To the west, where city fades and vanishes into the vastness of ocean, the sky is ominous and dark, unlit by the structures of man. Yet a powerful force of greater life, of nature, abides, still pushing in heavy clouds created from swirling masses of wind and rain in the northern Pacific. Again I observe so strikingly the endless hustling of people absorbed in their own worlds, somehow curiously out of touch with the presence of nature and the passing skies overhead. Though human consciousness continues to race ahead obliviously, it is indeed somehow inextricably, inexplicably, and mystically linked with the patterns of nature and the very light of the cosmos. Our human lives are finite, and life will deposit us again upon the shores of our own soul. Such is the rhythm of eternity.

From hustle to peace, from clouds to sun, from life to death, such are the patterns of our lives, the cycles in which we are all enmeshed.

So sleep, dear Grandfather, and release thy soul from the bondage of body. Rise. Transcend. Raise thyself unto those soaring heights far above the sufferings of this world. Rise, dear Grandfather, into death, into mystery, into that from whence all that is true and natural is born. Rise, dear Lazar, thou who hast laughed and danced and loved to the very end. Rise... rise... our love is with you. Rise into your victory, into your freedom, beyond the world and into the heart of the source of all. Until we meet again, Grandfather, you will be dearly, dearly missed...

Author's Note: As mentioned above, three months after the original writing of this piece, my grandfather was gone. He passed away exactly three years after my grandmother Miriam's passing, on the same date of May 16, and within minutes of her exact time of passing. During the writing of this piece and this particular afternoon I spent with him, my grandfather drifted in and out of conscious awareness. At times he seemed nearly comatose; while at other moments he woke, conversed with me, recounted historical events and happenings from his life, and was indeed present and lucid. He was an excellent storyteller and lived through incredible, dramatic world events, including WWI and WWII. Born with the name Lazar Velvel Mosh in a Jewish village (known in Yiddish as a shtetle) in Eastern Europe, his family immigrated to the United States through Ellis Island, New York in the year 1920, when he was a young boy. The family name Mosh was changed to Marsh upon entrance into the United States. His American name, Leo William Marsh, and the names of his parents and three brothers, are enshrined upon the historical Wall of Immigrants located at Ellis Island. Additionally, Leo and Miriam's eldest son, Robert, my father, had successful quadruple bypass open heart surgery on that very same date, May 16, exactly fourteen years after the passing of his mother and eleven years after the passing of his father. His heart was stopped for approximately one hour while he was connected to the bypass machine during surgery. May 16 is indeed a strange and unpleasant date for this particular lineage of the Marsh family.

Shells and the Sea

When I depart from this body
and embark upon my next journey,
gloriously engaging in what we mistakenly refer to as death,
just return this empty vessel—
the abandoned shell which will no longer be the temple of my soul—
to the place from whence cometh all shells...
the Great Ocean... mighty Neptune's crystal tear.

One Day

One day I shall awaken,
walk down to the sea
and enter into the Great Ocean
to swim away into my destiny.
I will not return as I once was
and I will not have died…
The great god Neptune,
one of my Mother's beloved sons,
is calling me back.
I am of his tribe.
I am of the Ocean.

Lo and Behold: The Passing of Buck

We've been visiting with death tonight
under the hazy, yellow glow of the full moon.
The moans of suffering
and wails of sorrow
fill the room,
and shatter whatever silence is left of this auspicious night
where hearts are broken
and a great soul is released.
Day and night,
light and darkness,
life and death
are colliding
amidst us.
Yet deep inside me,
in a mysterious, far-off place that I know little of,
the beaming of your smile
and the shining of your eyes
blossom…
bringing light into darkness.
Can your beauty soothe the sorrow and sting of death?

--2016

Terror at 33,000 Feet

It began with a sudden shake
as if an angry god smacked the 376 passenger 747 jumbo jet,
attempting to knock it out of the dark sky.
Then came the drop—
a split-second, thousand-foot fall
infinitely more steep and swift than any earthly roller coaster.
Stomachs and hearts hit the ceiling.
Shrieks pierced the serenity of the on-board dinner and movie.
Suddenly the flaws of this falsely disguised living room in the sky
were revealed,
its $250 million facade exposed.
Now, a den of terror,
a fragile collection of aluminum, plastic, and burning fuel
challenging and tempting nature and gravity
some six miles above the ground.
The *Fasten Seat Belts* lights flashed on.
Fear possessed minds so comfortable a mere ten seconds earlier,
as the shaking continued
violently.
Surely, the aircraft can't handle this.
We're going down.
This is it.
God help us, we're going down.

Another horrendous thousand-foot drop,
violent shaking continued.
Struggling to gather themselves
and maintain personal and professional control
the flight crew hurriedly pushed food carts from the aisles.

One rushed to the cabin loudspeaker.
"Please, everybody return to your seats! IMMEDIATELY!"
His refined British accent obviously stressed with fear and urgency.
"Clear the washrooms!" he continued.
The man sitting next to me—
his coffee spills, shaken from its cup.
Dishes rattle and fall to the floor.
Mothers reach for their children.
Eyes lock.
Suddenly we're interested in those around us,
as if we realize the importance of some brief human connection
in what may be the last moments of our lives.
I notice for the first time in six hours of flying
the people seated nearby me.
Indifference has turned to mutual shared experience—
connectedness.
I notice for the first time the color of the man's eyes who sits beside me.
I see his fear,
we connect silently.

Some turn to prayer,
"Mother of God, help us!"
Perhaps she will...
Others reflect on loved one's soon to be left behind.
Entire lives and personal histories flash instantaneously.
The most arrogant
are humbled,
the most atheistic
find faith.
This is the end.
Questions arise...
What now?
What matters now?

Was my life worth it?
What have I been doing for the past smattering of decades?
Who am I, really?
No longer is anything taken for granted.

Thoughts race, brows sweat, hands clench
stomachs churn in sickness.
Still the plane lurches violently
as if at any moment it will fall from the sky
and break into bits as it crashes into the cold sea.
This is the end.
This is the end!
O the terror as if to fall from a point higher than Mount Everest
through the dark night
and plunge to the bottom of a black sea
with several hundred screaming, maniacal people
terrified with the impending doom of the end of their lives,
the end of all they know, all they have, all they are.
One calls out aloud,
"Please God, help us! I don't want to die!"

Suddenly there is stillness, smoothness.
The violence is gone as quickly as it came.
Deep breaths, sighs of relief.
Then comes the captain's voice, ridiculously calm:
"Sorry ladies and gentlemen, just passing through a bit of turbulence.
Should get better from here on out."
That's it.

"Oh my God, we're ok. We're alive."
Numerous voices echo these sentiments.
A new appreciation for life is evident.
Passengers unfasten their seat belts
and begin to file by my aisle seat in the forty-fourth row

en route to the washrooms.
What have we learned?
How long will it last?
We know not what tomorrow or even the next hour will bring.
Perhaps our deaths are still just a moment away...
What an interesting commencement to my journey to the Holy Land.

--En route to Israel, 2000

Fifty-Five Minutes of Death

Rising higher and higher into the thin vaporous clouds
far beyond
the stability and security of the browns and greens of earth
the comforts of loved ones and friends
the beckoning freshness of ocean...
Higher and higher into the limitless sky
we soar...
Only the thunderous roar of jet engines
separates me
from the floating I associate with death
with the weightlessness of the soul's exit from the body...

The forested earth far below
blends into a series of checkered patchwork patterns
divided by highways and rivers...
Random houses look so small, the lives inside are like a remote dream.

Is this what death is like?
No longer can I touch the soft earth
or gaze into the eyes of loved ones.
I am separate
alone
floating and drifting through indistinct layers of cloud
through vapors scarcely condensed into form.
Up here, in fact, there is no form...
only thought, weightless like soul.
Spacious, ethereal, without density
as I recall my dreamlike out-of-body experiences have been...
somewhere in that realm beyond life...

My body seems almost useless...
mere skin, bone, and muscle strapped to airplane seat.
I am only thought
awareness
spirit...
existing beyond earth
momentarily beyond form.

I am the formless freedom of consciousness
passing through the vapors of both life
and death...

We vanish deep into the clouds now,
a gray darkness enfolds us.
My vision lost in colorlessness,
I exist in a world free from all contrast.
Now both sightless and bodiless
I have become even closer to pure consciousness.

Suddenly we burst forth from the lightless void of dark cloud
into the sun again.
Sight reborn
I delight in the radiant blue glory of sky
and the brilliance of the sun's rays upon a massive swath
of heavenly, white cumulus cloud...
a brightness far beyond any earthly shade
comparable perhaps only to the luster of the ocean's whitewater
under a tropical sun.

Turbulence comes...
this too I associate with death
with the soul's exit from the constraining physical chamber of body
with the spirit's process of freeing itself from the mortal pain

and material density of earth
to begin the journey to far-off realms
I know not where…

The airplane drops weightlessly,
shaking amidst the pressure of shifting air currents.
My stomach tightens and my breath ceases
but only for a moment
for I remember that I too am breath
in addition to thought and sight.
I wonder…
if in the soul's out-of-body voyages into those mystical realms beyond
if it does indeed possess a type of breath…

We pass by a double rainbow
cosmic hues of non-earthly color
luminescent
electric
again beyond the familiar realm of earth.
And then we begin our descent…
back to form, back to body, back to earth.
The patchwork designs of greens and browns
steadily focus into fields and trees
highways and automobiles
houses and people.
We land at last upon the solidity and stability of earth
and I am back to continue my work in the world
of being and doing
of living and loving.

This time
the experience of my death was momentary…
but someday, for all of us
it will be real…

and our soul's journey
beyond body
beyond form
beyond life
will begin...

Thoughts on Death

Death is but a transition
an exploration into a different aspect of our beingness.
No permanent end
as so perceived or believed
could such exist,
for that which I am never can be not,
and that which we are only more alive can be.
For what we experience now is but a dream
and death, the awakening to even greater life.

So mourn ye not in helpless man's guise
nor in strong man's false might
nor smart man's arrogance
nor laborer's toil.
Know that thou art like a tree
and your body ye shall cast aside
as branches their leaves in autumn.

To where shall I go in my time of autumn?
Tell you may I not
for thou shalt know in due time,
and words cannot unveil that which only Spirit knoweth.

Thus have ye faith!
and waste not another breath
on that which turns your stomach
or displeases your heart.
Seek ye that which falls from the sky in subtle beauty
and caresses the earth.
Walk hand in hand with loved ones

through the forests of God as leaves of life,
for our lives be such
and only be they such.

Let these words sing as a choir upon thine ears
and let the soft breath of life whisper against thy neck,
and may thou
and all thou knowest, seeist, and lovest—
live!
and only live.
For life is such...
the dream we are
the dream we always were
the dream we ever shall be.
Breathe deep
embrace the dream
embrace the dream
embrace the dream
and ye shall awaken...
Long live life.

--4:30 a.m., June 5

Thoughts on Death (Part II): The Whisper

Where goeth the whisper
after it is uttered?
Gone, is it?
Dispersed?
Lost for all eternity?
Where is the whisper
where is the sound,
in the sky, in the clouds
or in that from which it came?
Does one ever leave that from which it came?
Can life ever leave that from which it came?
Knowest thou the answers?
These questions that my heart asks to the day
and to the night
cry upon life as they kiss it,
bleed upon life's shoulder as they embrace it,
stab at life's heart as they long for it.
From life, cometh life,
to life, goeth life.
Death be there not.
Only life to be lived
and life to return to when thou hast lived.

"Whither shall ye go?" asketh my mother.
"I shall go to the place that designs the flowers
and births the stars."

And to my Beloved, what can I say?
What can words do
when fails my smile

to greet thine eyes,
when fail my hands
to caress thy skin and stroke thy hair...

--5:15 a.m., June 5

Author's Note: I woke early the morning of June 5 with a profound sadness, a deep longing for something incomprehensible to me at the time. I was overcome by a feeling that I would not be long for this world. Some swelling and strange formations on the top of my head were concerning me. As I explored this uneasy emotional state, I began to realize at its root was the fleeting and impermanent nature of our earthly journeys and my own fear and resistance to change and separation. Thoughts on Death I *&* II *were responses, reassurances perhaps, that came to me comfortingly from a deeper, wiser part of myself.*

Part Eight

The Seas of California

The Reunion

Ah, the Pacific!
My homeland waters.
It feels great to be back.
The rugged waters of the open ocean...
Ah, the beauty of the sun setting below the ocean...
The crisp, moist air coming off the shore,
the misty shroud of the hazy sky,
and the raw, splendid power
of this mighty ocean
and its surging
beautiful
surf.
I am proud to be of this water, of this Earth!
I am thankful to be home.

--Punta Canejo, Baja California, Mexico
Excerpted from *The Soul Rider: A Surfer's Perspective of the World* (1992)

A Glimpse of Nirvana

Pristine San Diego perfection... three days of radiant sunshine and brilliant blue ocean. Anchovies by the thousands... dolphins feeding everywhere and pelicans soaring and diving. In the afterglow of another gorgeous sunset, I dream and ride the orange seascape while pelicans soar just over head. I can feel their wings. The smooth liquid pulse, the breath, the glide... oh, total Nirvana!

--Leucadia, California

The Seas of California

The Seas of California call unto me.
The Seas of California call unto me.
The Seas of California call unto me.

In a sacred rhythm do they call.
In a sacred voice do they sing.
In a sacred manner
do they forever proclaim
the words of the Eternal:
"We are all One."

--Alejandro's Point, near Punta Santa Rosalillita, Baja California, Mexico
Excerpted from *The Soul Rider II: Neptune's Dream* (1995)

Three

Three mountains scattered across the land
like weeds.
Three souls scattered in the wind
like seeds.
Three birds floated in the sky
with the breeze.
Three veils lifted in the splendor
of the seas.

--Deep in the desert wilderness, Baja California, Mexico
Excerpted from *The Soul Rider: A Surfer's Perspective of the World* (1992)

Three soul brothers... *ALIVE*... amidst a Baja California transpeninsular surfing expedition, 1992. Left to right: Jason Appleton, Ari Marsh, and Eric Holland.

El Huerfanito
(The Orphan)

To the west, to the west, to the west
I am traveling.
Across the earth, across the earth, across the earth
I am treading.
Through the mountains, through the mountains, through the mountains
I am moving.
To the sea, to the sea, to the sea
I am returning.

--Solo journey, Baja California, Mexico
Excerpted from *The Soul Rider II: Neptune's Dream* (1995)

Surfing into the October Darkness

I surfed into the October darkness tonight... I could not leave the water after a nearly minute-long green flash at sunset thrusted me into a state of non-ordinary awareness. Everything seemed so pristine... and I watched the seagulls soaring out over the placid ocean toward the horizon where the final glow of sunset was quickly fading into the incoming night. The view from my vantage point, floating about in the dark sea, was dramatic, inspiring, captivating. I watched and wondered in solitude, with not another human around, sharing a rare, sacred privacy with the ocean as I waited for that last wave. To the north, I could see the lights on Coast Highway in Carlsbad, and the silhouettes of traveling automobiles, their headlights gleaming through the darkness. I watched even the traffic signals changing color in the far-off distance. The atmosphere was so clear and crisp that even Mount Soledad was visible to the south. At last, a dark wall of water rolled in from the deep. I paddled and rose to my feet. Curved reflections of light from homes atop the bluff bent and warped over the wave's surface as I sped across it. It crested and held itself open as I slid into a dry tube before gliding across the whole of South Reef and onto the beach. So grateful to share such natural beauty in perfect flow...

--Leucadia, California

Rolling Through the Eons

The afternoon aged.
The sun dipped into gold,
shining its deepening glow
upon the ever-changing sea.
A lone seagull hovered
then swooped down
carving the crisp air,
drawing the line of his life
across the scape of ocean and sky.
My eyes followed his smooth flight
then lost him momentarily
in the brilliant glare of the setting sun.

Masses of water shifted around me,
a tall surge approached.
Turning my board toward the shore
I stroked into the heaving wall of ocean.
It lifted me into its arms
and thrusted me out of its liquid nest
as a fledgling into the blue sky.
I flew across the sacred sea's magic surface,
carving it,
just as I had watched the seagull
only a moment before.
My arms rose from my sides, in balance,
touching the air as birds' wings.
And I was like the seagull
flying the mystical skies
of Mother Ocean,

drawing the lines of *my* life
upon the ever-changing sea.

Now
across the rocky shoreline I have trod
to stand humbly, in gratitude,
wet and clean, upon the tall rust-colored bluffs.
Far below
surges of water tirelessly traverse the vast sea
continuing on for eternity,
long after I depart,
long after my earth journey has concluded.

The last speck of sun gleams brightly
then dips below the curtain of ocean.
The eye of the day closes.
Night falls.
The lone seagull sits far off the shore
in the misty ocean
beside a clump of seaweed.
Life's mystical design continues...
ceaselessly
tirelessly
restlessly
eternally.
All perfect
all pure
all blessed...
rolling through the eons.
Ourselves,
as sparks of flame
rise up as waves from the sea,
take part in the great dance,

then disappear,
vanishing into the golden celestial void…
only to return again.

Always a wave approaches.
Always another follows.
Though all are enmeshed in life's synchronicity,
only few take the time to fly.

--Leucadia, California, October 1997

A Touch of Sea

Today I walked along the shore…
the smooth sea smiled at me
and its gentle movement touched my soul.
The flowing tide reached for me with outstretched fingers
and held my feet for a moment in its liquid hands,
then left me free again to travel upon my path.
The wind blew against my face and through my hair
and I breathed deeply of its invigorating, salty moisture.

I walked onward across the freshly soaked sand,
life came up from the ground into my feet and through my body,
the moist grains sighed as I passed.
White foam, a gift to the shore from the flowing tide,
rested in scattered clumps upon the beach
and blew in the wind for a moment
until it evaporated into nothingness.

--1994

The Green Flash

The last speck of sun
bright red and dancing
slips below the gleaming liquid horizon
fades into orange
then yellow
and erupts into a brief
fleeting
glowing green flash
before vanishing
behind the silky silvery curtain of ocean.

The Essence of Wave Riding

It's not that difficult to understand
if you're free.
It's rather simple, really,
and pure.
Man and sea.
Human being and nature.
The root is communion
harmony
joy.
The attainment
is as much one of finesse and sensitivity
as it is one of skill and talent.
It matters little what the equipment be
only that it is strong enough
to serve as a bridge
to connect rider with wave.

Whether this bridge, this instrument,
this vehicle we know of as a surfboard
be like a Stradivarius
or a beat-up '69 VW Bug
matters little.
For as we learn from the sparrow, the hawk,
the gull, the pelican,
there are many ways to fly
to soar
to be free.
Even the pigeon
who sits atop man's buildings
and wallows in his streets

corrupted by his spit, trash, and filth,
yes even the pigeon
with tarnished though unbroken wings
has moments of pure, free flight.
Just as Beethoven was deaf
a great musician can make most any instrument sing.
Thus our wings as surfers are diverse
for our instruments need only be in tune with ourselves.
The only requirement is that they adequately serve
as a medium
to bond, fuse, harmonize,
flesh with liquid
muscle and bone with sea water.

What matters most in wave riding
is the approach of the rider
his or her perspective, feeling, and level of sensitivity.
These are the crucial factors in communion.
The wild sea cares not who rides her
lest they come not to dance and love,
nor to create beautiful music
but to conquer.
For the sea, powerful in her might
cannot be conquered by man
and especially not by fool.

Communion is not ugly, nor awkward
but beautiful and graceful.
Hence the true wave rider
the liquid artist
knows how to delicately balance skill and knowledge
with love and respect
and has the talent and sensitivity
to meet power with finesse.

Empty, soulless skill is worthless
and under such conditions man and sea cannot commune.
One who has love but lacks skill is far better off
and more capable of communion.
And oh, true communion, wave riding at its finest
is wonderful art
beautiful music
sweet song.

When the crowds are gone
the scaffoldings collapsed
the cameras tucked away inside their dark, padded pouches,
and when the onlookers have gone home
never to return
and the investors have taken their money
and put it into the next fad,
there will still be those few humble souls
with finesse
alone with the sea
in joyful, peaceful communion.
Then, the essence of wave riding
its beauty
magic
simplicity
and purity
will stand naked and exposed before us.
It will be so deeply moving
that even the pelicans will appreciate our efforts
to match their masterful grace.

So whether it be a short, colorful stick of fiberglass
or a sixty pound log,
may we, as surfers, forever use our instruments
to connect the pure hearted

with the wild, untamable ocean.
For wave riding is
pure and simple
the art of communion.

Pure California Gold

Diamond shining
gleaming
blue water waves
peel across the sun-drenched beaches of soulful Leucadia
in North San Diego County.
I soar
and dance
along these feathering liquid swells
adorned with glistening sunbeams.

O, to dart in such a manner
across the oceanic spectrum of time and space
while the planet revolves and orbits the sun...
while the moon's gravity pulls the tides...
while stars implode and explode
and the universe itself expands,
ever engaged in flux and movement.
Yea, I travel
though not far in apparent physical distance,
merely across a wave upon a stick of fiberglass
yet to sublime mental and spiritual destinations.

Born of this diamond draped sea
I am.
Born of this sacred, bejeweled sea
I am!

Gliding upon these smooth and perfect waves
I come to know myself again
as the sun begins its descent into tomorrow.

My classic 1970s single-fin surfboard
is now the superb instrument
of my presently uncaged and newly freed soul,
the two fused together harmoniously
through the grace of my youthful flesh.

Aye, to dance and paint upon the stage of water,
to live a dream while yet awake,
to experience the glories of heaven while yet on earth.
In fact, to leave the earth and let the human die,
to live, to fly—for a time,
like pelican through air
like porpoise through water.
To cast one's otherwise marred identity
into the delicate flames of water
smoothed with gentle, warm sunlight.
Ultimately, to change oneself,
never to be the same again.

It is in these moments
that I come to know my Self,
my nature, my purpose,
if only for the superconscious moments of my rides.

Again, to leave the earth
and become more than human
more than amphibian,
a creative being who dances upon the ever-moving water
like a living god.

In this sun-glistened ocean
was I born.
In this land where waves break over shifting sands,
where light and motion play as one,

have I found pure California gold.
And in the delicate, yet radical movements
of board upon wave,
of bright yellow rail upon smooth blue ocean
have I experienced life at its fullest.
For here upon the ever-rolling, ever-recurring,
time-tapered swells of moving water—
energy traversing sea and thus forming wave—
man is elevated to pure physics, atoms, particles,
once again consciously and perfectly enmeshed
in the cosmic scheme
of Creation.

Upon these diamond shining, gleaming, perfect
blue water waves
that peel across these ancient, sun-drenched beaches...
I am.
Hear me life,
I am.
Hear me life, for I am here now.
Hear me life, for I am you.
Hear me,
hear me,
I am!

--Leucadia, California, May 2001

Part Nine

From the Lips of the Divine

From the Lips of the Divine
(I dreamed the world...)

I dreamed the world, the sand-covered world.
And would you believe
that each grain—every single one—
is completely unique?
You can wander My deserts
and comb My shores for Eternity,
but I tell you—
you will never find two grains of sand
that are entirely alike.
You can wander My fields for a lifetime,
and likewise,
you will never find two grains of wheat, or rice,
that are the same.
Infinity exists.
You are there!
You are in the Land of Infinity—
the land of infinite ideas and endless possibilities.
You can call it God, or Heaven if you like.
I simply call it Life.

Everlasting Ripples

Our lives are fleeting
like the raindrop
forming in the heavens
and falling speedily toward the earth,
a single drop in the cosmic sea.
As quick as the drop hits the ground and shatters into infinity,
our journey through life is over—a mere instant.
But as the drop that falls into the sea
creates everlasting ripples as it returns to its source,
so do our lives create ripples
in the pattern of evolution and human consciousness
as we return to ours.

Thoughts from Eternity:
The Kumeyaay Village

The desert...
It never ceases to amaze me.
How long have these rocks been here,
how long has this sand blanketed the dry earth,
how many eons has the sun cast its scorching glow
upon this valley
and the wind bellowed its lonesome call
through these canyons?
Thousands... millions... billions of years...
The never-ending timelessness of this world is seen here
felt here
experienced here
now...
Change—
does it exist
or is this mighty land resistant to the laws of life
and death—
aging, decay, and rot?
For it is said that the nearby oasis is drying up.
But this desert—
'tis already dry,
what can be taken away,
sunshine?
Yes, the people are gone
but this land knows life without people.
And in a moment I will be gone,
but what am I to this place?
This sacred land has played host and hostess
since the birth of time

watching, sheltering, feeding
insect and bird, lizard and snake, dinosaur and human...
This land has always been the giver, the provider.
So what are the several decades of my life
to this place?
What can my life mean
to a land that has seen the birth and death
of stars
and has given of itself to trillions before me?
O, but not much do I ask from this great land
but to live with it, love it, feel it, taste it
for the duration of my short journey
upon its back...
for in a moment I will be the very dust and sand
upon which I momentarily rest.
And I cry out to life
I cry out in love and gratitude
for what I am to you—
your child.
So let me rest my spine upon yours,
caress your warm sands with my fingertips,
bathe in the light and warmth of the sun,
for soon I will be gone
and this stunning, ageless world will still be here...
just as it is now.

The author, amidst a fleeting moment of celebration and gratitude in the Anza-Borrego Desert, California. Photo by Linda Lobbestael.

The Great Sea of Energy

All things move in the great sea of energy...
The energy is everywhere...
in all things.
It is infinite
and all-encompassing.
Feel it within you, around you,
in the air, in your blood.
In China it is called Chi.
In India it is known as Prana or Shakti.
In the West, some simply call it energy,
while others refer to it as life force,
and yet to others it is Spirit or God.
It matters not what you call it
just that you acknowledge it
are grateful for it
and cultivate it within your self.
Do not doubt that it responds
or that it exists
for it is the all-permeating life substance
and it can be directed at will by he or she who loves enough.
All things move in the great sea of energy...

Whispers from the Beloved

I am a Poet
wandering the cosmos
singing the song of life.
Like a firefly, I flicker.
Like a sun, I gleam.
Like a shooting star,
I dart across the dreamy landscape of life,
dancing in glory to all who look up.
Far and near I roam
during my brief sojourn through this celestial sea.
Other worlds call me,
and soon I shall go
to sing my song in even stranger lands.
The cosmos is O so large.
And though I am but a mere whisper
in the voice of the Great Poet,
my poems nonetheless
contain Her very sweet breath, Her soft voice,
Her timeless smile, Her sincere gaze.
We are all Her Poets,
and our voices, in sadness and in joy,
are Her whispers.

From the Lips of the Divine (Part II)

I dreamed the world.
It is a thought in my mind.
One small thought.
And each of you is a part of that thought…
a pebble cast upon an endless coast…
a grain of sand upon the shoreline of eternity.
Grains of sand, amidst grains of sand, amidst grains of sand…
one of them is you.
But I tell you *not* that you are small and meaningless,
but that you are great and magnificent.
Each one is like a seed
in the center of a beautiful flower
that waves and sways in a field of a million flowers.
And this world, really, is a land full of flowers,
though many not yet in bloom.
And within each seed is the capacity to create another flower
with a dozen more seeds…
and from each of those new seeds
shall come more new flowers,
each with a dozen more seeds.
For this is a world of infinite possibilities and endless variations.
The cypress, the pine, the redwood—
all came from tiny seeds.
Why, within each needle of the pine—each sprig of the cedar—
lies an entire world.
All born from that one thought (not even my greatest thought).
So my little grains, my precious seeds,
sprout into your fullness.
Rise in glory from the beautiful sand-covered earth.
Give life to the world.

As part of my thought, it is your gift—even your role.
Wave your hand, and create a million flowers with a million seeds.
Flash your smile, and cast myriad beams
upon the ripe canvas of earth.
Why, the very ground will form flowers beneath your feet...
if you only remember that
I dreamed the world.
It is a thought in my mind.
One small thought (with a billion tangents).
And each of you...

Hands

I looked at my hands
and stared deeply into their veins
and saw immense life…
such intricate, incredible life
which I have never quite noticed before.
Pulsating, living, growing, moving, ever-changing
are my hands…
filled with veins, blood, cells, and bone.
And to think, I can control them with a thought.

The One Within

I looked into the mirror and gazed deeply into my reflection…
After a time, my image began to blur
and it faded into soft glowing radiant light.
As my sight sharpened,
a new image faced me
and I stood looking into the eyes of an old man.
Though advanced in years
his face shined with a youthful vigor.
Light danced in his eyes
and his smiling bearded face beamed with wisdom.
He smiled and spoke,
"I am your Infinite Source,
draw upon me at all times
for I am you
and we are endless."
The image blurred,
dissolving into blazing colored light
so bright it forced my eyes closed.
When I opened them a moment later,
I again beheld the familiar reflection
of what I believe and perceive to be me
but now know is not,
for the vision
and the feeling
of the Ancient One within has remained…

Dialogue with the Soul

"O Wise One
deep within
I ask you…
Where does the tree end
and its roots begin?
Where does the sky end
and space begin?
Where does the wave end
and the sea begin?
Where does my toe end
and my foot begin?
Where does my body end
and the living planet Earth begin?"

"O Human Son,
I am the beginning
and I am the end,
yet that which I am—
which all life is—
is both beginningless and endless…
Never has life been not—nor ever can it be not.
Beginnings, endings, divisions, separations,
exist only in the minds of men.
For as one of my many Sons explained long ago,
'I am in you,
you are in me,
and we are all together in the Father.'
So you see who you are
who you always have been
and who you ever shall be,

once you remember
once you re-realize your Self.
There is no separation between the root and the tree,
nor the earth and the stars,
nor you and the rest of life in the universe,
nor even the Son and his Father
nor the Father and his Mother.
Nothing is separate.
There is only One.
Everything is One.
Thus, you *are* me
and I am you
and we are all forever..."

Circuit N

There's a circuit that exists in our bodies
and in the universe...
It's called Circuit N.
Ancient mystics have told us that the N stands for nothingness.
The circuit, within our bodies,
if tapped into
runs energy into a vacant region of the brain
at the back of the head, near the crown.
The destiny—
the final destination—
of all energy traveling upon Circuit N
is a minute pinpoint in the upper rear of the brain's parietal lobe
one-tenth the size of a pinhead.
This tiny location
is capable of swallowing massive amounts of energy
and transmuting it into pure light.
Circuit N
erases
all human-imposed consciousness from the energy that travels through it
and completely reprocesses it
turning our thoughts, fears, beliefs, hopes, and dreams
into nothingness.
Once the energy reaches the final destination
and is transmuted into pure light,
it is then flooded in dynamic split-second surges
throughout our entire bodies.
If one accesses Circuit N
one can erase his or her entire identity
merging with and thus becoming pure universal consciousness.
The key to accessing Circuit N

is to follow the neural pathways of the brain
as it responds to and processes the ultimate meanings of three words—
nothing, never, and nowhere.
When one accesses Circuit N
and reprocesses all of his or her consciousness into pure divine energy,
it is said
that afterward he or she will have forgotten even the very of existence
of the circuit itself…

Children of the One Great Light

Don't you see?
We are all children of the One Great Light.
We share the same parents
who some refer to as Mother Earth and Father Sky,
but they are One, and so are we,
regardless of language, race, religion, creed.
Everything is One.
Nobody here is any better or worse
than anyone else.
Hear me as I speak my heart to you,
for I am passing on this knowledge, surrendering it,
sharing it
as it was passed on to me by the Creator.
You see, this knowledge is not mine,
it cannot be owned, it cannot be possessed.
It can only be shared in love...
And I know that times are hard and you are troubled,
and faithless
but you must keep your heart,
for we are all brothers and sisters in the colors of life.

Cycle

I am like a flower in bloom.
With smooth, steady ease I gain in brilliance,
with smooth, steady ease I gain in strength.
Life's power is guiding me,
life's power is teaching me.
In due time I shall open my dazzling petals unto the sun.
With nature's care I grow in color,
with nature's care I grow in beauty.

I am like a fruit ripening on its vine.
In measured rhythm my skin softens,
in measured rhythm my heart sweetens.
In the dry winds I shall grow to my maturity.

My changing is constant,
my changing is graceful,
my changing flows like a stream
meandering through the canvas of nature.
My season of harvest is soon to be due.
I shall fulfill my purpose.

Soon after will come my withering.
But I am not alarmed,
for as my budding is like the sunrise
so too is my wilting like the sunset.
Each is just as beautiful and glorious.

My pace is peace and my path is eternity,
like the sun across the sky.
For within the pulse of creation,

within the timeless beat of the cosmos' own heart
I abide forever.

Sprout

You are a seed
dropped by the Tree of Life
into the infinite sea of the universe.
We are all seeds
cast upon the eternal soil of life,
scattered across the pastures of the universe
by the mighty hand of Cosmos.
Seeds, seeds, seeds
cared for and nurtured by the Grand Gardner's overflowing love.
In due time shall we sprout
and fill the Almighty's Garden
with our love and joy.

The Garden and the Rose

Your gentle petals blush under soft morning sun,
your brilliant colors deepen in hue.
O rose
in your prime
in your hours of life,
standing gracefully,
stately postured as Queen of the Garden.
Your perfect shape
trimmed and trued
by nature's hand
of warm sun and moist earth.
Drops of morning smile in your eyes
your sweet fragrance laughs.
Kings and princes flock to your side,
praising your beauty
and resting in the spring grasses
beneath your slender trunk.
O my love
thou art the rose of my life,
for thee I shall gladly give my tender skin
unto thy thorns.
But time hast thou not for me
for in a different garden do I grow
only to gaze at thee
in the pleasant sorrow
of distant admiration.
And so the gardens bloom
and the trees of earth bear glorious fruits
of beautiful color,
and the tall, thin bodies

of fresh green grass
dance joyously in the wind.
And the seasons demand of me my growth.
My stalk thickens,
my leaves broaden
and I grow strong.
Boldly I reach,
stretching my limbs
toward the heights of Infinity.
And no more do I see thee,
for control the garden can I not
and only my own branches can I prune.
And other queens rise and take shape
each with unique beauty and subtle graces,
and in kind company
amidst tender gazes and silky smiles,
my memory calls my thoughts unto thee.
But the sun's heat has thickened the spring air into summer
and my leaves have begun to wrinkle.
And beneath my cloak of brightly colored guise,
my brittle stem splits.
And through the wind
I hear your call
of wilted petals and withered stem.
And though my heart yearns
to respond to your cry,
the grasses have gone to seed
and the earth has browned.
And though my roots maintain their vigor
and cling deeply to the soil in which they have burrowed,
my limbs weaken.
Time has stricken me in its heartless obedience
to the seasons.
And though fate is beyond my grasp

I still smile,
for the buds of my tomorrow rest dormant.
And though a precious part of my tender heart has died
in the Grand Gardener's sweltering summer fate,
I know that spring shall come again.

A Lesson on Vision

The oaks stood tall and bold, their branches extending out toward one another, their leaves joined together as if they were holding hands. On the ground, amidst the moving shadows of branches and leaves swaying in the breeze, stood a small group of people.

They gathered together, as though they were one, forming a half-circle and staring intently at a man who stood alone facing them. He was a strange-looking man who stared blankly into the trees, yet he stood firmly and with an air of dignity. He had just finished speaking when one of the gatherers stepped forward. It was a young man, secure in himself, though he knew himself not, for never had he searched.

"Do you suffer?" asked the young man boldly.

"No," replied the strange man without a doubt or hesitation. "Not in the way that you mean it," he continued. "Does the sparrow suffer because it does not fly as high as the hawk or have the wing span of the eagle? No. It accepts its lot in life. It remains proud, even in the eyes of death. And the fruits of the apple tree," he continued as he raised his hand in gesture to the nearby orchard, "are no less sweet if they come from the smallest tree in the orchard, and they may even be sweeter. Each tree stands alone and always with dignity."

The strange man paused as a gust of wind rattled through the oak and cottonwood leaves. He tilted his head slightly as if listening to something of which the onlookers were unaware.

"There are reasons and lessons in everything. My life is an opportunity for new triumph. Suffering exists in one's thoughts. One chooses whether to suffer or to rejoice," concluded the strange man.

"But you don't know what a flower looks like," said a woman compassionately.

"And you can't even see the trees," added another of the gatherers.

"Oh, but I can," responded the strange man with a smile. "I see them with my hands, and with the sensitive tips of my fingers. How many of you have caressed the bark of a tree and read its bumps, or felt its grooves? Each tree has its own story to tell, for each one grows in its own unique manner and lives with its own individual perception.

"And I see with my nose and ears as well. Each tree sings a different song when the wind blows through its leaves. Each rose has its own distinct fragrance.

"I see and feel things with my mind—in ways that most of you can scarcely imagine. I see beauty, individuality, uniqueness... and in some of you who stand here before me, I can even see your pain, your longing, your sense of isolation.

"But most of all," continued the strange man, "I see life with the eye of my heart. And this is the true blessing of my life. Too many of us are restricted to seeing solely with our eyes. This often leads to a false sense of vision, for the eye of the heart sees far beyond the eyes of the face. And if I could see with my eyes like the rest of you, then perhaps in the eye of my heart, I would be blind."

His words rattled off as the wind had done so through the leaves, carrying a clarity and wisdom beyond explanation. His message was rich with the sap of truth, and it permeated the forest, dripping from thin green leaves, echoing amongst strong branches that touched and held one another. The strange man was right and they knew it.

The gatherers remained in silence, pondering his words as a profound stillness filled the air. He had given them new insight into their lives, their pain, their sorrow. As they began to disperse back toward their village, the strange man walked deeper into the woods and disappeared into the shadows.

from Shivaratri

verse I

i have touched the realms
where god and goddess abide as one
bodies and kundalini merged in union...
i have tasted that sacred kiss
like rose petals upon my lips...
and I have felt you there
amidst it all
with chants of Shiva filling the air...

and though here I abide
in this that is now
a world with structures and forms that keep me from knowing you
feeling you
breathing you...
a world where machine-like timing and the logic of intellect rule
over the rhythms of heart...
i shall say
it matters not
how vast and endless this universe is...
nor does it matter
how many countless embodiments come
and go...
or in what various forms or distant worlds
i may abide...
for I will find you.

suns will be birthed
other stars will dim and die

eternity shall span its endless breadth
and yet
beautiful divine sacred woman
i shall find you
i shall find you
i shall find you
somewhere
in some land
in some time
i will find you again
and the moment will be ours
free from boundary…

verse II

i remember the taste of that most sacred kiss…
the sweat from your skin
the wetness of your mouth and lips
that most sacred nectar of the goddess…
it is the essence of creation itself
that which the hummingbirds seek
and the honeybees feed to their queen…
the most delicate precious sweetness
within the heart of earth's rarest flowers.
you dear goddess
are that very essence…

thousands of years ago
i worshiped thee…
and thousands of years from now
in future days
in unknown lands
i, as living god

shall worship thee again...
and from your sacred nectar
the sweat on your skin
the moisture upon your lips
the light in your eyes
the dew from your spirit
i shall spin entire universes into existence
i shall spin entire universes into existence...

One Soul

You... me... all of us...
We, the brothers and sisters of life,
are weaving a tapestry
a great garment
woven with the threads of our love
by the wills of our soul
and the needles of our concentration.
United by the stitches of our commitment,
we dance together
to create a textile rich in color
and flavored with the delightful spices of each one's uniqueness.
And when our work is completed
we shall drape the whole world in our blanket of love,
and together, enfolded in the crests of our devotion
we shall cross the threshold of eternity,
for we shall be One Soul.

A Promise

The Swede, the German,
the Jew, the Mexican, the Buddhist,
the Iranian, the Christian, the Syrian,
the Samoan, the Nigerian, the Indonesian,
the Russian, the Cherokee, the Muslim,
the Nicaraguan, the Korean
all join hands
embracing
not only one another
but Unity.
In the clasp of their hands
there is a promise...
like the texture of sand dunes
blown smooth by desert winds...
like the skin of a newborn,
soft, supple, innocent...
like the turquoise splendor
of a mid-afternoon ocean,
and the ten billion diamonds of shimmering sunlight
that sparkle upon its breast...
there is a sweetness...
like one that only the sun can bring
to the choicest fruit in the orchard.
The promise is one of respect
of understanding
of tolerance
of brother and sisterhood...
of shared affection.
The promise is one of love.

Part Ten

An Ephemeral Radiance

La Gente de Guadalupe

Vast are we
like the mountainous earth
having bold peaks that reach toward the heights of the sun
and deep canyons that rest in the shade of cool breeze.

Fresh are we
like fields of grass bathed in sparkling dew
ever-changing in colors of green and gold
and blessed with the recurring flowers of spring.

Deep are we
like the boundless sea
mysterious and eternal
beyond knowledge.

We shimmer beneath the sun
carrying in our hearts a billion dreams
and living in our infiniteness a billion lives.

--Cañón de Guadalupe, Baja California, Mexico, 1996

Merge

From the lost coast
atop the highest peak
I look out over the vast ocean.
Endless land meets timeless sea.
Giant rocks rest as scattered islands
boldly they interrupt the never-ending pulse of waves.
Smooth swells greet the rocky headlands
and burst into powerful white foam.
It is here where my attention rests—
in the breaking waves
in the churning foam
in the impact of water upon rock.

And you?
You are like a dream vanishing before the misty glow of sunset.
Your image dances before my mind
your purity and grace hold my heart.
Were you ever real?
Far away
the setting sun dips below the placid horizon.
Golden shimmering heaven awaits.
You are there, I know.
Maybe tomorrow I will join you.

--Cape Blanco, Oregon, 1995

Thoughts from a Liquid Twilight

Streaks of cloud
delicate orange and pink-hued
float
hovering over twilight's golden band,
the western void
where only traces of solar light remain.
My attention rests there
in the emptiness of the sunless sky
where colors deepen
soon to lose themselves into the darkness of night.
Ten thousand waves I have ridden across this shoreline
where the rush of tide and the hiss of feathering swell
have been my rhythm and my song.

It's different now.
Everything is different
since the hut.

My thoughts meander…
roaming skyline and seascape
as I wait for a wave
amidst the shifting colors of another dusk.

Who would dare to compare the whirring of car engines
and the buzzing of freeway noise
to the sound of the ocean?
"It's all white noise,"
they have told me.
"Nonsense,"
has always been my response.

My heart is raw…
painfully raw
and so vulnerably exposed to this life, this world,
this insanity, this beauty…
Only the ocean knows the truth of the salty water
that drips from my eyes.

A wave approaches,
I turn and paddle…
Rising to my feet I hear her voice in the soft crash of sea.
Oh, her voice
her beautiful voice
its gentle, musical pitch
like home
or nirvana…
I don't know of a more perfect sound.

I'm doomed…
even the ocean
my ocean
the womb
the place that birthed me so many countless times
and has held me
and will hold me
until I die…
Yes, even the ocean speaks to me of her.
Or perhaps she speaks through it.
Has she always?
I don't know…
the lines are blurred.
Everything is different
since the hut.

What is it about this hut?
What happened in the hut?
Hmm…
a taste of her sweetness
a meeting of hearts…
Damn it!
The hut!
I'm doomed…

Though distracted,
I nonetheless negotiate a fluid bottom turn
and project onto a seamless wave face…
my hand slides along under the fold of a hollowing tube.
Oh, this is good…
riding waves again,
lost in the liquid glide I know so well.

Colors are darker now.
Does she see this—
this dying day
as she races along the freeway?

Would I trade this—
this glorious natural beauty
for the white noise insanity of freeway
to be by her side right now
amidst traffic
stacks of school papers to be graded
the distractions and realities of career
relationship
routine
and the balancing of passion

with aging,
of happiness and personal truth
with societal demands?

Would I trade this—
this moment of ocean and heavenly sunset
for freeway chaos—
to be with her?
A thousand times throughout my life I have asked this same question
and each time the answer has been the same...
except for tonight.
Tonight it is different.
Everything is different
since the hut.

--Leucadia, California, October 2010

Within You, Within Me

My heart spoke to you all night
embracing you while you slept...
sometimes speaking in words
whispered from my lips into your ear...
sometimes speaking through touch
my warm hand across your back
a stroke of my fingers through your hair...
sometimes speaking in silence
a breath, a sigh...
always the language was of closeness
of connection
of sweetness
of depth
of the experience of beauty, awe, love...
savoring the preciousness of this fleeting moment
of togetherness...
for now as I write this you are gone...
yet my heart still speaks to you
with every beat, every pulse
I am with you... I am with you... I am with you...
closer than breath...
inside you
in your body, in your heart
in your bones, in your blood
and you equally
within me...

--2014

A Shattered Dream

After you left
I realized that the Hand of Destiny
had shattered my dream.
I searched the ground where we had stood, lived, shared, and loved
desperately looking for broken bits and shattered pieces of my dream
but I searched in vain.
And in my deepest moments of gloom, despair, and utter darkness
I realized that this was all okay
and maybe even a blessing...
for this that I have lost was not my only dream
nor my last.
I have many more
some of which are far more beautiful and fulfilling
than you...

The Agreement

I awoke from my final dream
lying not in my bed
but sitting upright, legs crossed
upon some vaguely familiar shoreline.
I opened my eyes and saw you there
the setting sun lighting your face with the fiery glow of twilight
your hair deep shades of auburn and black.
I closed my eyes
to relish in the bliss of your company
then opened them again and you were gone.
My heart sank into that all to familiar feeling
of aloneness.

I remembered the agreement I had made with life…
and all too soon a harsh wind roared up from the churning sea
and raged against my face and body.
I sat
motionlessly absorbing its fury.
Behind me was a tiny space of sand
sheltered from the terror of the elements.
The gulls crowded there, against my back
to hide from the roars of wind and water.
Crashing waves tumbled in the cold ocean
frothing waves howled with the wind
screaming…
screaming…

Devastation

I saw you this morning
from ten thousand feet...
amid the gray suburban sprawl
of Los Angeles.
The roaring of the jet engines
drowned my moans
burying them into the silent, lonely depths of my heart.

I saw you this morning
from ten thousand feet...
you and city
cradled by brown rolling mountains
limitless sky and unexplainable sea.
The airliner rocketing high
my nose pressing to the cold, lifeless window.

I saw you this morning
from ten thousand feet...
my cheeks wet with tears
as I strain to grasp the vanishing view of home.
Your cries and pain
spiraling like seismic waves
throughout Hollywood
and West LA
across Venice Beach—
where we sat yesterday with heavy hearts
watching the windblown surf.

I saw you this morning...
in the blur and confusion of heartbreak.
The shrinking sprawl of Southern California
growing fainter.
The places where we walked, lived, breathed
played music, sang, loved, grew—
all disappearing from my sight.
All that we have been
now lost in that hazy cognitive emotional stew called memory.
All that we ever were
now a mere part of that vague ambiguous murky realm
called the past.

I saw you this morning...
in the passing glance of a flight attendant surveying the aisles...
in the wandering eyes of a woman sitting behind me...
in the disappearance of my homeland below
as the jet airliner continued to climb the sky ever-higher
on its journey toward tomorrow.

I saw you this morning...
in that obscure middle ground between heart and mind
where we live only so briefly
swirling betwixt our thoughts, emotions, dreams, imaginings
and our reality.

I saw you this morning...
as I soared away to another land
another time
another life.

--En route, eastbound via commercial jet, leaving California

Homeless Man, 1982, West Los Angeles

In a world molded by mechanistic thought,
where industry, machines
and the grand agendas of corporations
rule over the human heart and spirit,
he meanders aimlessly through the soiled streets,
searching for sanctuary.
Hopeless
with ragged clothing
he rests his head on an empty forgotten
rusted-out newspaper sales rack
on a dark lonely street corner.
Collapsing at last onto the concrete
he feels its harshness
its inflexible unforgiving nature,
and he smells the soot, grime, and filth
of the city
in his face.
He pulls an old newspaper
over his shoulder for cover
as he curls into a ball and tries to sleep.
His eyes close
and for a moment he drifts off into a dream…
He is at home, together with his love
in a warm bed awaiting sleep…
A roaring bus sweeps through
the late-night city streets
and awakens him from his fantasy.
A tear falls down his cheek
and drops into the gutter
where it joins a million other tears

and a river of spit and urine
on the long journey
through the sewers
to the sea.

Homeless Man's Prophetic Dream, 1976, West Los Angeles

⎯⎯ᴄ⎯⎯

Running... running... running!
Running desperately in a concrete maze
I breathe deep and hard of the spoiled air,
trying to get away.
I'm sick and drunk with pollution in an artificial hell.
The long boulevard
crowded with buildings and shops
offers nothing I need
nothing to ease the pain of my separation
my isolation...
Automobile horns scream
while plastic people proud of their image
smoke sticks of cancer as they wander the strip of cement
that suffocates the earth below.
Defeated... exhausted...
I fall onto the ground and crawl onto a tiny patch of earth
from which a lone tree, blackened by soot and smog,
protrudes its shriveled stalk into the man-made hell.
I kneel on the dirt
screaming for earth, screaming for nature, screaming for life.
Frantically I dig down into the earth
reaching for the roots of the tree.
Digging... digging...
deeper and deeper until I grab the roots
and try to pull myself with all of my might
down into the heart of the earth, under the ground,
to get away from the toxic hell.
Screaming... screaming!
An oblivious passer-by flicks a still burning cigarette onto me

and mumbles, "Crazy bum—get out of the dirt."
A burning sensation explodes inside me.
Mouth wide, face dripping with sweat, eyes bulging...
I awake screaming, heart thumping wildly,
beside my wife, in our warm bed, in our comfortable home.
"It's okay sweetheart, it's just a dream," she says softly,
without the faintest idea of what would soon come to pass...

Stone in My Heart

This morning I woke
not with a joyous song in my heart
although I have known those precious dawns…
but with a stone lodged in the center of my chest.
Though the stone was beautiful to the touch,
smooth and polished,
it was heavy
and as I sat up in my bed it pulled my heart down into my stomach.
I noticed first the terrible nausea
the wrenching, clenching darkness in my stomach.
I thought surely I would vomit up my very heart
and stain my sheets and pillow with blood.

I know who put the stone there
and how she put it there
but what I repeatedly question is why.
Her smiling green eyes and bright beautiful face
her long sandy-blonde hair
her slender figure
and turquoise halter-top…
She shines
she shimmers
she dances
she beams…
and she stabs open hearts with her deceptive beauty and tenderness
then places cold, heavy rocks there
while one is vulnerable and deep in slumber…

So the day has unfolded…
the afternoon has come
and the rock is still lodged in my heart
which is now somewhere in my stomach.
And I keep wondering…
How many times can love crucify me?
How many times can life kill me?
Don't you know, life
don't you know, love
I'm already dead.
Every wound now just drives my death a little deeper
into that mysterious void of darkness.

The Illusion of Hope

Hope slipped into my room tonight
casting a warm glow upon a once barren and desolate plain in my heart
she brought a melody
barely audible
yet it colored the silence with a quality of promise
albeit remote and intangible

The warm glow and the melody
together
which Hope brought—
as she slid through cracks in the wall
cold crevices where despair and grief had shut out everything
but themselves—
provided a comfort that I had not experienced in far too long

I opened my eyes wide to behold her
my face almost smiling

Hope has braids I tell you
and smooth, dark skin
she possesses an ancient beauty
with the moon in her eyes

But as I reached for her
in the darkness of my own night
from the seemingly endless woods through which I had been treading
lost and alone
she slipped back out again

through that very crevice from which she had entered
for she was Hope
and not Love

Thus Hope
clad in blue dress with dark braids
crept out of my world tonight
vanishing as quickly as she had come
disappearing before even the slightest connection could be experienced
and taking with her the warmth, the glow, the melody
which she had brought
leaving me again in a land of utter desolation

Departure

Through the fog
through the mist
through the rain
and into the splintered sunlight
filtering through tall Appalachian forests
we have come.

Through fear
through insecurity
through doubt
we have moved.
With commitment and communication
we have come to this place at this time...
we have come to this moment.

Two anomalies
journeying
moving closer
searching
for home, for meaning
exploring those universal divine energies
of Mother and Father...
amidst comfort and longing
independence and fear
excitement and grief
to glimpse a momentary loss of self...
a mystical meeting with a deer.

Identity-less
without roles
without expectations
without mirrors...

Will the falseness of form
the desires of ego
shatter for us
if we abide
clothed perfectly
balanced securely
amongst Mother and Father energies
without expectation?

Can we abide
identity-less
in our own beautiful mysterious unimportance...
in our own deepest, most simple nature?

--Asheville, North Carolina, 2005

The Finding

Born of wind and rain
I come to know myself again
amidst the crisp fresh air of a winter's night.

Cleansed
to the soul
of the societal implants of fear, suspiciousness, doubt, insecurity
and their bitter fruits
confusion, exhaustion, disillusionment, hopelessness...

In a world so gorged with useless information
computations, social expectations, endless deliberations,
financial stratifications...
it is easy to become lost.

Lost...
amidst the hands of a clock, the lanes of a freeway,
the numbers on a credit card...
Lost...
for who among us truly knows who he or she is?

But at last, for now
I am found...
found by the invigorating winds and welcomed rains
of a December night
found by the great powers of nature
found by a truth that transcends humanity and the world we've created
found by that which reminds me of peace

of life
of who I am...
and who I shall be.

Yet perhaps tomorrow, or next week
I will become tainted, corrupted, again...
but in the raging sea
the howling, whirling winds
the midnight rain...
or atop a sage-covered slope of a California hillside
or in the midst of the fragrant pines of Cuyamaca or Laguna
or through the mist of a salty breeze blown upon me by the dancing sea
life will find me...
always, and again, life will find me.

In the end
not a one of us shall be left for naught
for even in the darkest, most confused, lost corners of this world
even in the anguish of societal hells,
the wind, rain, and sea
the free-ranging skies of eternity
the true powers of life
shall indeed find us.

Shadows in Madrid

After a while
when the day fades away
there are only shadows
only shadows remain…

And the hustling world
and the city lights
all close down
for they were never real…

And so we grow and live
and take and give
and soon we are gone
but the shadows remain…

And on we go in our race for existence
to see and live
to do and give
to share and taste and laugh and cry…
we rush to have and to collect
we live to own and play to win
we do and see and do again…

But in the midst of my hustle
I stop and wonder
And as the leaves of life
fall gently down upon me
caressing my world
I smile
and I am…

and for an instant
I am not doing
but being...

And I see my fleeting world
and the needless haste
and I slow down
to a smooth flowing pace
and relate to the world
with tenderness and grace...

And for now I see beyond this world
and I know that soon
this fleeting existence will be gone
and only the shadows will remain...

--Madrid, Spain, 1993

This Place

When I sit down and try to make my mind work
it always leaves me in the dirt
and takes off to a place far out of reach
where there is no government.
Nature flourishes from the ground
colors of peace are all around
but then I snap out and see the light.

And so I'm walkin' down the street
what do I see?
Some uptight politician
hustlin' by me.
I say, "Hey, Mr. Senator,
won't you please slow down?
Don't you know there are people dyin'
on this here side of town?

"This place is full of poverty
little children crawlin' up to me
askin' for a piece of bread.

"This place is full of bigotry
whiteman's ignorant sense of superiority
kickin' black folk in the head.

"This place is full of hatred
our children couldn't escape it
you ripped away their peace pipes and love beads."

But he didn't listen, he sped right by
looked my way with his hand held high
I swear I caught a glimpse of a dollar sign in his eye.
And so I look to the people for a final plea
because the price of life—it should be free
whether it's the life of a person or simply a tree.
So tell me, are things the way they oughta be?

So stand back and take a look, you blind fools
and quit following your absurd rules
of a plastic society in a nuclear world!
Wipe that make-up from your eyes
and clear the smog out of the skies,
and allow a little light to shine upon you.
And for once in your life
look through the gray
and see the blue.

A Million Thoughts

I am a book
of a thousand pages,
each with its own side
its own truth.
Each story, each sentence
is different
depending on that
which is of the reader.
Each page contains hundreds of words
thousands of letters,
twist them around
and they can say and mean anything.
Read me…

The Love Box

Past, present, future
swirling in the mystery of this single moment
this encounter
this mysterious now.
Even amidst the fading light of day
the incoming night
and the dark gray ocean in the distance
still her eyes are lit
aflame.

Twenty-six year-old love letters
at last opened again from an old shoebox
their hidden magic exposed once more
to the open, sea-infused air.
Unseeable particles, like fairy dust
waft around us
floating, hovering.
"I love you…" they whisper.
We inhale it—
their fragrance, their magic dust.
Once lost potency stirred and ingested anew
inseparable now from the oxygen in our lungs,
our bloodstream, our hearts.

Her lips
here before me
flush and ripe with color
yet cast upon folded, time-weathered page in decades-old pink lipstick.
There they are.
There she is—now

yet then.
What is going on?
Where are we?
When are we?
Or perhaps, simply, "are we?"

Handwritten letters
bedecked over and over again
with that most un-understandable, non-comprehensible word—
"love."
Other words and phrases too awaken
from these past, once lost pages—
"forever..."
"I miss you..."
Laughter, tears, passion, dreams, anger—
it's all there—
here!
Yet where?
And once again, when?
Now
or then?
And how long...
truly... how long
is "forever"?

--Real Dove Line, Los Angeles, California, 2013

Flowers at My Feet

The world is dropping flowers at my feet...
It began with a single rose petal
pink and purple-hued with a brilliant yellow center
nearly heart-shaped
it waited for me silently, wordlessly
upon my doorstep one morning
and welcomed me into the new day.

The following week it was a charming yellow daisy...
It graced my porch one afternoon
and greeted me with a flutter as the breeze blew across it.

Interesting... strange even...
there are no signs of potted plants or flowers nearby
and my second-floor apartment
is both high above and quite a distance away
from any neighboring shrubs or bushes.

I don't know what I've done
to deserve the world dropping flowers along my pathway...
perhaps she knows I need it now—
these subtle reminders from nature—
for great challenges have descended upon me
and my path through the dark woods has been long and steep.

I'd like to think that a mystical fairy is responsible for these flowers...
a delicate being with wings who tends to gardens
and sensitive hearts.
Or perhaps the placement of these flowers
are the simple deeds of a marvelous angel or deity

who watches over me
guards me
blesses me
protects me...
Or maybe
these special flowers are symbols of love
from a beautiful female admirer...
and she is both carefully and consciously dropping them along my pathway
as a sort of gift...

This morning
it was the most lovely pink and violet-colored flower
an offering from a Hong Kong orchid tree
although I have no idea where there is such a tree nearby.
It was lying on the pavement right beside the door of my car
and had a message for me
something ephemeral which I couldn't quite grasp...
a reminder
about love
and hope.
I picked it up and placed it on the seat beside me
as I drove off and into another day.
I wondered again about the messenger...
the fairy
the angel
the deity
the woman...
and as my thoughts
drifted off into the clouds and incoming rain
I had the most subtle inclination
that these various recurring flowers at my feet

were the handiwork of the most mysterious, invisible messenger of all—
the wind.
Which brings to my mind another question...
who or what controls the wind?

--2016

Looking East...
Thoughts on Lovely Torture

⟍⟍

Like you
when you're here,
I am always looking west
towards the ocean,
focused on what's happening on the coast...
the water, the waves,
the sand and rocks of the shoreline,
the ebb and flow of the tide...
I dream off endlessly towards the sunset.

Now, today,
I find myself looking east,
from where comes the rising sun.
I gaze out across the expanse of blue sky...
over the trees,
beyond the roaring highways
and bustling cities,
even over the vast mountain ranges of California...
in search of you.
You with the sea in your eyes, in your face,
in your hair, in your body, even in your name...
you are east,
for now.
And thus today
I dream away towards that wild and barren Arizona desert
and its collections of humanity...
where it feels as though somehow part of me now abides,
brown and dry,
yet so colorful and lush with you.

The Ghost Walk

With an accidental flip of the garbage disposal switch
the 4 a.m. silence
is shattered…
it roars with the ache of our separation,
echoing through the sleeping village of dreams…
She
is
my
dream…
laid out upon her back
with eyes closed,
blissful smile stretching into sleep.
With scratch marks on my body
I quietly close the front door and slither out into the darkness,
a ghost
a phantom
known by no one
except her.
The highway is deserted
and I float across it, almost bodiless,
as in dream-state.
Everything is quiet.
Everything—
but our two hearts,
for they rumble and thunder
with the passion and sweetness of our love.

I Am Myself

I am myself…
My soul's truest companion.
My own sincere light from within
will never fail me,
and it is the only thing
that I can truly, completely count on
in this world.
I am.

Part Eleven

On Dolphins and Humans

On Dolphins and Humans: Questions About This Fleeting Life

It was in the middle of a surf session with a good friend when those familiar questions surfaced in my mind... those questions about life purpose and meaning... about the goals of our society, the values of our culture. I began wondering, as I often do... How did it all get so complicated—these lives we lead—the demands, the complexities, the busyness... What have we achieved, what has humanity truly achieved, and at what cost? Oh these dreaded unanswerable questions that, at times, possess me. What is a meaningful life? How do we balance health, connection, and inner fulfillment with financial demands, social expectations, and material pursuits?

For far too many years, I have followed a different path, responded to a different calling, and sought rhythm and harmony with the sea. But there is a price for a life such as mine... the price may be loneliness, on occasion... or a lack of stability, or security... for mine is a simplicity that many would deem inadequate. We all have choices to make...

What have I to show from riding countless thousands of waves... for immersing myself in the ocean for literally years of my life... for pursuing a dream... an intangible connection to nature, to ocean, to Source...

Like the Tibetan Buddhists who, with great patience and peacefulness, create elaborate mandalas out of colored grains of sand, only to scatter them into nothingness upon completion—an act symbolizing the impermanent and ever-changing nature of our lives—so have I created my own temporary, sacred mandalas upon the smooth blue ocean through dozens of years of riding waves amidst the gleaming Southern California sunlight. Each movement upon the water is a prayer from my heart, a celebration of joy, or a soft cry of suffering amidst this life struggle.

What defines or measures a successful life? Is it quantitative, such as the amount of wealth or property one acquires? Is it based around ownership? Or is it qualitative, and based upon intangibles that cannot be measured or exacted upon the finality of one's life journey? Why are we here? And what of our culture, our ideals? And what of my seeming lack of cooperation with the social norms that we are apparently bound by? Where abides a nonconformist's life, such as mine, upon the spectrum of success, happiness, and achievement?

This particular day, as my buddy and I surfed one of our favorite local reef breaks in Leucadia, California, these questions haunted me profoundly… and answers seemed nowhere to be found. We were the only two surfers in the water and the solitude afforded much time for quiet reflection and deep introspection.

Several days earlier, I had been speaking with another friend of mine who had shared with me that he felt trapped in his current life. The demands of family, providing for his children, and the amount of money needed to keep up with the life-path that he and his wife had chosen, had all proved to be too much to handle. They were behind in their mortgage payments, had racked up credit card debt, and the stress was taking its toll on their marriage and family life. Both he and his wife were deeply unhappy, and they argued often over finances and decisions related to their future and the well-being of their children. "I've fallen into a trap," he told me, "and I don't know what to do." At one point, while we brainstormed possible solutions, or at least actions that would perhaps ease the struggle and the tension between he and his wife, he blurted out, "Jeez man, I'm fucked. There's no way out." He calculated that in fifteen years his youngest child would be finished with college and then maybe the financial pressures would ease. "Fifteen years…" he reiterated discouragingly.

Fifteen years in the life of a man or a woman who is unhappy, miserable, or dealing with an uncomfortable, stressful situation is an unfathomable duration of time. Even fifteen days of intense stress is enough to compromise one's immune system and debilitate one's physical health to a point where a full recovery may take several months or more. Why do we, as Americans or Westerners, live the way we live, and who professes that it's the correct way? Why are individuals such as I deemed irresponsible or unsuccessful by some because we have chosen personal well-being and inner fulfillment over bustling bank accounts and retirement funds?

Several years back, a neighbor was having a party for his son's tenth birthday. I was informed, in advance, that those attending would consist primarily of his son's friends and their parents. "You may not want to come," he had told me, since I was, at the time, both single and childless. It was an interesting period in my life. I had just resigned from a tenured position teaching elementary school and was soon to turn forty. I had recently sold a house that I had once owned with my now ex-wife, and had made a personal vow to "buy my life back." At the party, I began conversing with a guy about my age. He told me that he was there with his wife and two children, both of whom were friends with the birthday boy.

"How about you? Which kids are yours?" he asked me, gesturing toward a crowd of screaming children.

"Oh, I don't have any kids," I answered.

"Really?" he responded with surprise. "Well how do you and your wife know the Madsen's?" he asked, searching for more information.

"It's just me," I responded. "I'm not married."

A series of questions followed, and thus I, somewhat hesitantly, began to explain my situation. I shared with him that I was not only divorced, but I had just sold my house, quit my job, broken up with a recent girlfriend, and was about to depart on a six-week journey all over California, surfing, hiking, writing, and camping in my truck.

"Wait, let me get this straight," he said in bewilderment, "you don't have any kids, you're not married, and you don't even have a job?"

Oh gosh, here we go, I thought to myself... *here comes the judgment and the subconscious jealousy that often results in a slightly degrading comment or two. Stay peaceful,* I told myself in preparation for what was to come. *Stay calm, be compassionate.* But what followed was not only a complete surprise to me, but without a doubt the most honest words I had heard the entire afternoon.

"Damn, you're so lucky!" he exclaimed. Indeed, we all have choices to make...

My buddy and I were paddling back out to the line-up after catching excellent waves that peeled all the way to the inside of the reef. To be more precise, we had actually caught the same wave, but surfed it in different directions. In surfing, this is known as "splitting the peak." A wave crests up, like the peak of a mountain, and each surfer takes off on a different side of the peak, thus riding the same wave in opposite directions, one going left, the other going right. A large wave loomed in front of us as we paddled back out toward the empty line-up. A gorgeous, liquid blue wall rose and began to heave, when suddenly, from within the depths of the wave itself, a huge dolphin burst through the heart of the wave and began gliding across the smooth wave face a mere twenty feet away. This majestic creature, seemingly for pure joy and thrill, surfed across the entire length of the breaking wave and disappeared into the tube, the hollow interior of the wave, right in front of us. Simultaneously, my friend and I erupted with primal shouts of celebration, knowing that we had not only witnessed something beautiful and remarkable, but were a part of it.

Dolphins have been called the original surfers, and the stories of their extraordinary intelligence are beyond inspiring. While bottlenose dolphins thrive along the California coast, glimpses of them in the ocean are always special. As surfers, we know and understand, perhaps on some mysterious biological level, that they are indeed wise and compassionate beings worthy of our greatest respect. Bottlenose dolphins not only have larger brains than humans, but recent scientific research suggests that they have an extremely developed neocortex, the part of the brain responsible for self-awareness and problem-solving (Grimm & Miller, 2010). Studies have shown that they have the ability to transmit cultural knowledge across generations, teach one another to use tools, and to communicate through an elaborate system of whistles, pulsed sounds, and complex body language (Bottlenose dolphin, Wikipedia). Further, they have repeatedly demonstrated a highly evolved level of both emotional intelligence and memory.

Obviously, dolphins live very different lives than the majority of us humans. While we constantly prepare for the future, they seem to exist in the present moment. While we manipulate our external environment to fit our needs, regardless of negative impact and outcome, dolphins seem to keep harmony and balance with their oceanic habitat. They have no possessions, no stockpiles of food hidden in underwater caves... they have no property, no systems of ownership, nor do they have supplies for future emergencies. They have no mechanical or automated transportation, no computers, no cell phones, nor any need to get on-line. They have no money, no electricity, nor even clothing. They are pure, natural beings, living lives virtually in complete harmony with nature; and it may be crucial to our own survival that we don't discredit or demean their example.

We looked for the dolphin after the wave had passed, but he or she had gone. I thought of my friend who felt trapped in his current life... and the married man who called me "lucky." I thought of the people whom I had lost... people whom I had loved very dearly who either didn't agree with my lifestyle and choices, or those who simply did not feel that I could provide them with, or at least contribute to, a level of financial security that would support them in feeling both safe and protected.

We all have choices to make... and there's no rule that says humans are right and dolphins are wrong. Only opinions can draw such conclusions. In any case, I am so grateful to know the ocean as I do... to be able to share moments like this with a good friend and majestic creatures who inhabit this beautiful planet along with us. In spite of all of our social, technological, and material achievements, nature and its highly evolved, non-human beings have something profound to teach us about life on this earth, and about the value of simple, natural living.

And while I still don't possess the answers to the questions pondered at the beginning of this story, I can say that we all have a life to live and to reflect upon. It's a rather short life... that comes and will soon go. It arrives for a time, like sparkles of sunlight upon a wave, and then vanishes. We all have choices to make... some of us live modern human, or twenty-first century Westerner... others live tribal man, nomadic man, or gypsy... and perhaps even some of us live a little bit of dolphin.

Author's Note: Special thanks to my good friend and fellow soul surfer, Jason Weber, who shared this remarkable experience with me at North Reef, Beacon's, in Leucadia, California.

Part Twelve

Land of the Sun: Poems from Alta and Baja California

Land of the Sun

I come from the land of the brown dry earth,
the land of the chaparral.
I come from the deep canyons
where brush and thicket hide rabbit and lizard,
where coyote roams and fox hunts.
I come from the dry coastal foothills
in whose face shimmers the blue Pacific.
This is my home and I am proud,
forever I am proud.

I come from the land where the ocean sparkles,
the land of the eternal summer,
the land called California.
It is my home, it is my heart.

I come from the land of the wide sky
where hawk and vulture soar.
I come from the land of the Chumash,
the Diegueño, the Cahuilla, the Kumeyaay.
I come from the land rich with life and heart
where the fragrances of sagebrush caress the air.

I come from California,
the soul of the world
where the freedom and vastness of ocean
meet the strength and purity of earth.

I come from the land of the sun,
the golden land
where sandstone sea bluffs guard the shore

and well-worn trails wind through twisted canyons.
I come from the paths that lead to the sea
where the pelicans glide and the seagulls race.

I come from the land where the santana winds
blow the brilliant sea into turquoise.
This is my home, this is who I am.
This is my spirit.
Honor this land, respect it,
respect me.

I am a man of sincerity and peace
and I am proud, yet humble
and ask nothing but to live in my home,
this land, the golden land,
the land of the sun,
the land of my spirit.
Hear me,
for I am this land
and it is me,
forever.

Pink Flames of Sunset

At sunset
the birds fly west
to the sea.
They follow the sun
to the fresh ocean
and soar along beaches soaked with salt and seaweed.
They rise high
into streaks of color
born in the golden hour.
In freedom's flight
they glide toward the horizon
where they disappear
into the pink flames of sunset.

--Del Mar, California, Summer 1996

Punta

Unceasing, immeasurable, pure, immaculate
coastline.
Endless beaches and cliffs
twisting in unimaginable ways,
forming jagged edges and coves
and razor sharp points of land
which wrap inward further than the eye can see.
The ocean... turquoise and beautiful,
sparkling to the horizon.
The land... ancient and wise,
unaltered by human forces
continually shaped and molded
by the breath of evolution.
Uninterrupted processes of change
artwork
which nature has spent eons to craft.
Gently, impeccable, patiently
monitored by water and wind.
I walk along
pondering infinity at my fingertips,
enthralled by the vastness.
I follow the path to a thin stream of sand
which blows from a cliff in a soft breeze.
I watch the sand rain gently down onto the beach
where it forms a giant hourglass.
I lay on the hourglass,
countless grains of sand
finely ground into a bed of infinite time.
Eternity is within my comprehension.
I am lost in the instant of the moment.

Pure living,
free from numbers on a clock
or deadlines.
Simply the slow paced, perfectly balanced laws
of nature.
I am one with the total perfection of the moment.
I have discovered nature's peace
and I know it will prevail.

The Timeless Land

Trekking across the dry, hot sands of eternity
amidst sweltering heat and blazing sunshine...
Sweat seeps from my brow
pouring down my face
dripping down my back.
The elements insist on cleansing me.

Parched shards of lava rock show faded reds and browns,
fragments of volcanic explosions many thousands of years ago.
I bend down low
to gaze closely and behold the magic
of these solidified slivers of once melted rock.
A stream of sweat falls from my brow
and trickles onto a few of these ancient pieces of eternity.
The fresh dew of my being casts a watery shine
and once faded rocks sparkle,
brilliantly reflecting the sunshine,
seemingly rejoicing in the liquid love
of which they have for eons been deprived.
In a moment, however,
the shimmering drops of sweat have evaporated
and these old rocks are again dry and pale,
languishing in the harshness of living countless centuries
in this desert.

I stand up and look eastward, toward the horizon
and out across the gleaming Sea of Cortez
whose liquid essence captures beautiful shades of color and light.
Sparkling blue and alive,

unchanged throughout millions of years of evolution on this planet.
Outliving all.

I gaze westward at distant peaks,
brown and barren
yet host to numerous species of plant, insect, bird, lizard, snake—
even coyotes and pumas abide here.
The mysteriousness of these mountains is captivating,
there are no humans here.
Hundreds of feet in the air
seven vultures circle atop a majestic peak.
They ride the breeze
just as their kind has done since its origin.
Out here the will to live must be painstakingly strong
or survival is not possible
but the harsh, dry climate, the barren lands, and rugged terrain
give rise to mysterious powers
and strange facets of life and existence.

Once again I walk,
trekking across the dry, hot sands of eternity
amidst sweltering heat and blazing sunshine…
Sweat pours ceaselessly from my brow
bleeding from my skin
watering the crusty earth.
As I journey onward
for a moment I feel one with the timelessness, the mystery, the solitude
of this land…
If we could but realize what a brief instant it is
that we walk upon this earth,
we would waste not even a moment.

--1994

Waterfall Canyons of Borrego

Crystal waters
cascading downward
with gravity's force
through sheer granite cliffs
falling into a pool of nature's fresh clear life-giving substance.
Nearby in a dried fork of the river
just north of a small spring
lies a bed of white sand...
dry earth sweltering under a hot sun.
Broken pieces of pottery
are remnants of a people
who lived before.

--Anza-Borrego Desert, California

The Great Stone Faces of Palm Canyon

Giant formations of rock
form Great Faces
some ten humans high.
Eternal Stone Faces
dignified, wise, ancient
possessing a stern patience
a proud humility.

Weathered and shaped by wind, water, and the hand of time
they appear more alive and alert than many people I know.
I sit in awe
and gaze into deep, penetrating eyes
set above high cheek bones
a wide, protruding brow
falls into a granite nose that extends outward
like the beak of an eagle
then tapers off above large lips and a strong chin.

This image
made of stone and earth
is quite Native American in nature
and reflects a powerful relationship
with the crystal streams and palm-lined canyons
of the Borrego desert.
Though silent, it speaks of an ancient knowledge
unknown to the people of today
yet held sacred by the once flourishing Cahuilla.
This is a face of honor and courage
like that of a great warrior or leader.
This valley knows his people well.

Smaller, boulder-like formations of rock
protrude from the mouth of another Great Stone Face
they spill out like words from his lips.
One can almost hear and feel
the rumbling of these mighty words
as if they are the wise council of a great chief to his people.
Perhaps the distant drone of the waterfall
or the ceaseless churning hum of the stream
secretly utters these frozen syllables.

A chaparral bush
protrudes from a crack below his eye
forming a solidified teardrop.
Perhaps he mourns the loss of the beautiful people
who once inhabited this magical canyon.

Above rests the face of a protector of this sacred land.
His eyes are stern, even fierce
showing an unyielding determination
to keep his dwelling place eternally pristine
and uncorrupted by invaders.
Something at which he has, for now, succeeded.

Did these Great Faces model themselves after the Cahuilla
who inhabited this valley for thousands of years?
Or did the people, over time
come to adopt the facial features
and grow into the likeness of these Great Faces?
Visions of Aztec ruins
guarded by powerful beings
carved into huge masses of rock
flash in my mind.
Are these giant rocks which lay before me
the faces of Gods

of Great Beings who live or once lived?
Perhaps they are the protectors and caretakers
of this lush, desert oasis.
One thing I know,
thousands of humans have come and gone
from this scenic, palm-lined canyon
yet these Great Stone Faces have remained
reflecting the wisdom of their timelessness
and emanating an ancient peace
of which much of the humanity of today
knows not.

--Palm Canyon, Anza-Borrego Desert, California

La Sierra de Mágica

"Across that ridge and in the valley beyond," spoke the old man as he feebly raised his hand in gesture, pointing toward a distant mountain range, "there lies an ancient, sacred village, not yet corrupted by the modern ways." Thoughts darted across my mind like monstrous birds in a gale wind—the heat was getting to me. For three days I have traversed these mountains—alone. Now suddenly an old man appears from the heart of the rocky earth and tells me of an unknown village. Am I delusional?

I stared at his face, wrinkled and extremely weathered from years of hot sun. His gaze was piercing and frighteningly honest. The dryness in my throat suddenly vanished. Who is this man?

"The people are one with the land, direct descendants of the oldest of native cultures in all of Baja. Go there, mi amigo," he continued, "for you have much to learn. An old Indian waits for you now. He looks much like myself, you will know him by the sparkle in his eyes."

I gazed at the distant mountain range. Giant faces in the tall peaks beckoned me with smiles. On a flat-topped ridge stood a tall, solitary cactus. Its outstretched limbs appeared to be calling me onward.

I turned back to the old man, but he was gone. Silence hummed deafeningly in my ears. I reached for my bottle and nursed my dwindling supply of water. I looked back to the sea of white sand over which I had trod. Throwing my pack again over my shoulders, I began the hike across the desert toward the distant range. Onward, into the reality of the unknown…

Author's Note: This piece was written in the early 1990s during an eight-day, solo sojourn into the wilderness of Baja California. To me, it captures some of the essence and mystery of the Baja experience: the solitude, the vastness, and the wild unknown. In addition, it touches upon some of the deeply fascinating people who inhabit the peninsula's most isolated outposts, many of whom possess an enigmatic balance of wisdom and superstition.

Villa Jesús María

I saw you, my brother
in my dream
you were young and pure
from many years back.
You were meek and spoke softly.
I see you now, my brother
in my mind
you are unhappy and bitter.
Your eyes are filled with anger and hatred,
you are living death.
And so I ask you, my brother
"Que obtienes de tus problemas?"
What have you from your problems?
What have you from your troubles?
What have you from your battles?

--Villa Jesús María, Baja California, Mexico, 1992

The Cirio Tree

Cirios stretch upward from the dry, barren landscape
towering strangely over the crusty, waterless land
with curious strength
and twisted flexibility.
Over rolling desert mountains your colony grows eagerly.
Under fiery sunshine your kind flourishes.
I gaze in awe at your agelessness
your ancientness.
O strange and deathless boojums
undefinable botanical wonders of Baja
much can we learn from you.

Cirio Tree (Boojum), Central Desert of Baja
California, Mexico. Photo by the author.

Purification

As I walk, I stare down at the pure white sand
bleached by the sun over millions of years.
My feet sink deeply into it with each step.
The beach is eager to meet a new soul,
it has been very long since a human has set foot here.
Shells stack on the shore
faded and brittle from countless days of sun,
colorless like the sand.
Remarkable lone strands of green life protrude
from the dry sandy earth
but the mighty ocean, 'tis full of color and life abounding
yet under the same sun.
And I walk, leaving naught but a trail of footprints
until the tide swings in to greet me
and washes everything away into nothingness.
And soon I will be gone, my body dried and parched into dust
as the rocks and shells into sand.
My footprints erased forever,
without a single trace that I had ever come.

--Baja California, Mexico

California's Himalayan Peak

Majestic pines and cedars reach high into the heavens
stretching up the face of the giant god
known as Shasta.
But beyond the tree line
where its surface is barren but for broken rocks and cracked shale,
the true magnificence of this sacred mountain
beams in splendor.
The brilliant purity of snow blankets its higher elevations
even in the warmest months,
while crisp, clean air begs to purify all who trek upon its back.
Atop its most glorious summit, some 14,000 feet above the sea
there are no mysterious Buddhist monasteries
where colorful Tibetan prayer flags wave in the icy breeze.
No golden-bronzed statues of the Buddha
observe the terrific silence.
No smiling monks, clad in colorful robes
watch over the world below.
Yet rumors abound
of a group of trans-dimensional beings,
enlightened masters
who have perfected themselves in ages past.
They inhabit the sacred mountain, it is said
where they pour out great currents of light and energy
to help and guide weary mankind.
Many centuries ago
long before Europeans inhabited the Americas,
the local native people believed that their grand Mount Shasta
housed the Great Spirit.
Perhaps they were right.
For certain, it is mysterious, powerful

and inspires in the heart and mind of the seeker
the very boldness of nature
and the possibility of transcendent consciousness.
Its mystique is ever so intriguing.
Its purity is ever so transforming.
Its beauty is ever so engaging.

--Mount Shasta, California

Mount Shasta, Northern California. Photo by the author.

Spiritual Dreaming

In the Mount Shasta vicinity, the spectacle known as Sunset provides a gateway for mysterious, heavenly meditations of ever-changing shades of light and color upon nature's wilderness of ancient, ever-receptive tapestries. A feast for the eyes, senses, and heart. Spiritual Dreaming. Who are we, and where are we, or rather, where in the vast universe is this spinning planet we call home?

View across Lake Siskiyou in the Shasta corridor, overlooking the surrounding mountains and the western sky. Photo by the author.

Big Sur

Behold the land
where massive cliffs fall away into the immense Pacific
where the always cold sea pounds against slippery rocks
where tall redwoods reach into the misty sky
amidst rolling chaparral-clad mountains...

Behold the place
where Highway One twists alongside one of the most scenic
and obscure coastlines in the world
where otters frolic in rich kelp forests
where California gray whales pass so close to the shore
as to be detected by sleek foxes and quiet deer...

Behold the land
the mountainous coastal strip
where poets and artists escape to reflect and create
where Southern California materialism cowers
before the bold hand of nature
where phones, clocks, and televisions become insignificant—
swallowed up by natural forces so grand and immense
as to inspire even the numbest of minds...

Behold this uncorrupted stretch of sanctuary
where flowing brooks hush and sigh
as they spill into the raging ocean
where hawks and eagles soar above mist-shrouded hills
where awe-inspired couples sit upon empty beaches with clasped hands...

It is a place of journeys, of expeditions, of nature walks.
It is a place for soul searchers, for friends, and for lovers.
It is a place to be alone
and yet united with life on the deepest of levels.
Behold the enchanted land
the beautiful, mountainous coast
of Big Sur.

--2002

Part Thirteen

Ari-isms:
Random Thoughts
and Aphorisms

Ari-isms

Not strength, nor knowledge, nor riches can hold back the break of dawn or the flow of time.

Each rock, pebble, and grain of sand holds the mystery, magic, and vastness of the universe.

There is no beginning to the magnificent dream of the cosmos, and there will never be an end. There is only a "now" and it is forever.

You are eternity, clothed in a fleeting conglomeration of stellar dust and saline waters, carrying your electric current.

There is an unexplainable essence that abides within all things, connecting everything like a strand of beads, uniting all things into a precious whole.

Each of us is capable of great miracles. What imprisons us is our disbelief, our unawareness, and our fear.

In the silent palace of the human heart hides a treasure greater than any wealth known to man. It is the secret of the soul. May we all feel and know the magic, beauty, and perfection that abide within us.

May we face our days of life and death with the wild bravery of that which is natural and free.

The tragedy of human existence is that the majority of us have forgotten one of the most basic principles of life on earth: interdependence.

Once I was a dream in the mind of my father,
then I was a seed in the womb of my mother,
now I am a sprout in the garden of Earth.

Dream… seed… sprout…
Roots… branches… leaves…
I am all, and have been since the beginning of time.
I am forever a cell traveling endlessly
through the bloodstream of the universe.

The fine point of my concentration is the tip of the needle pulling the thread of my existence through the fabric of modern life.

From the instant the glorious morning sun peeks over the eastern horizon, it is slowly, silently, sleekly stalked by night.

Rather than kill two birds with one stone, I choose to feed two birds with one seed.

Place on this earth the seeds of love, so they may grow strong and spread their fruit to all living things.

Intelligence ought not to be measured by the quality of one's words, but by the quality of one's message.

Arrogance is a form of ignorance.

Education ought not to teach us what to think, but how to think for ourselves.

Social popularity and fame do not equate to happiness and fulfillment.

Although the mind can exist and thrive, to a degree, in the world of virtual reality, one cannot so easily fool or manipulate the body. The body exists in the material realm, the realm of physicality, as do the trees, flowers, fruits, mountains, and rivers of earth. We must not ignore the physical sufferings of our planet and its various life forms by attempting to delve ever-deeper and more exclusively into the illusions and falsities of various on-line social media and virtual realities. Nature cannot be cheated. The earth, and our living bodies, depend on daily physical interaction and the sensitive touch of real hands.

When I turn off my mind and feel the silent peace,
poetry flows through me with grace and ease.
When I sit with a pen in my hand and try to think,
I stumble and fall and trip over the ink.

Is not the "om" of the yogi and the "moo" of the cow one and the same sound?

Guide me, Father, for I am dumb, but do not call to me for I am deaf, and do not appear to me for I am blind.

Often the pain is greater for the one who causes harm, rather than for the victim; for the swords of guilt and sorrow plunge deep and sting wickedly.

Bless the poor soul who suffers in the turmoil of hate and anger, for there is nothing worse than a soul who cannot find love in the heart.

The universe that we know of did not begin with a bang. Nay friends, this grand spectacle began with a delicate, soft exhalation, yet of such cosmic, gigantic proportion that flaming suns and brilliant, translucent worlds were spun into existence. Everything that we experience now is an echo, a reverberation of that first, original divine breath.

Our galaxy is but a speck of dust on a windswept plain in a far-off region of the universe.

If you think you are grand and important, take a moment and gaze into the heavens.

Become fine, like the sands of the desert...
become smooth, like the sea-polished rocks of the shore...
become graceful, like the winged creatures of the sky...
and you will learn the secrets of harmony and flow.

The flower of my heart is the treasure of my soul.

Breathe the stream of air, for it is the balance of life.
Become one with the river of life, for it is the natural flow.
Sing the song of silence, for it is the music of the soul.
Be at peace, for turmoil weighs heavy on the heart.
Tranquility is the key to the doorway of harmony.

Remember detachment,
for that which you cling to
will someday become like water and slip through your hands.
Remember illusion,
for that which you think to be certain
is often only fleeting and temporary.
Remember gratitude,
for that which you take for granted
may be stripped away from you.
Remember love,
for life cannot exist without it.

Do your good deeds for the silence of your heart alone and not for the praise
from those around you. And those achievements which you have made,
whether within yourself or in the world, do not boast of nor cheapen with
publicity; but carry on silently, knowing of the good in your heart and in the
hearts of all beings, and herein you shall find your reward.

In the stillness of the moment all shall be revealed... Gravity, water, wind,
earth, power, freedom, silence...

A human being who no longer dreams is like a bird with a broken wing.

My mind is my wing and each thought a feather. They can carry me to the highest heights of freedom, or plunge me into the darkest depths of insanity.

Beware of what you hear through the grapevine, for it yields distorted truths.

All you have is your state of mind; think wisely.

Perhaps there is only one "four-letter word"—HATE.

Your life is like clay and you are the sculptor, the artist, capable of molding and shaping your life, creating of it whatever you desire it to be.

You stand atop the pinnacle of your knowledge, gazing boldly across the colored skies toward the higher, distant summit of your freedom. Love is the trail that must be trodden to reach your destination.

Each of us is a poem written by God upon the canvas of Earth.

Each of us is holy in the eyes of God,
not one of us is any more or less so.
Each of us is a stone,
being smoothed and worn into our fineness
by His mighty tide,
and amidst our tumbling
we come to rest upon His sacred shore
by His sacred sea.

When up is down, take a plunge into the liquid sky and swim amidst the dreamlike, watery clouds of your imagination.

Los Angeles... the city of my birth and childhood... Sometimes I feel it to be a tragic mixture of broken dreams and human beings trying to become something. Yet just above the rush and haste, the mockingbird sings on a quivering electrical powerline, and crows cackle and soar, heckling us, mischievously questioning our actions and values. Sure, the creative spirit thrives, hope is alive, and the human heart is filled with goodness and beauty... but seriously, let's look around. What are we doing and why? What are we bent on achieving, or becoming, and at what cost to our humanity, our integrity, and our planet?

When Man has chopped down his forest, he will find himself roaming amongst dead trees.

Cages, zoos, factory farms, slaughterhouses… My, oh my, what are we doing to the beautiful creatures of this earth? What insanity has led to such wickedness?

"Sometimes love is just not enough," she told me. She was indeed correct. It is a simple reality that to some people money brings a comfort and a security that not even the most nurturing human warmth can compare with.

So perhaps the Beatles were wrong… and money *can* buy love… and love is *not* all we need…

Hmm…

Interesting that love, loyalty, and genuine connection seem to be of less value to many of us than success, social popularity, and financial security.

Sigh…

Sometimes I look around at this world we've created and wonder how everything got so entirely fucked up. Other times I look around and see such immense beauty.

Deep breath...

Human beings, at least in Southern California, are becoming creatures that walk around with a little electronic device held in their hands at all times. Often these creatures don't watch where they're walking or look one another in the eye, but instead have their faces buried in their little device and their fingers running across it incessantly. Perhaps the sky, the trees, the birds, are wondering what has happened to us, and why we no longer look around and take in our surroundings? What would we do with our hands, our minds, if we could no longer clutch our little device? Perhaps we'd touch a tree, or hold someone's hand. Who are we becoming and why?

The key to your freedom lies in your willingness and ability to allow your personal identity and its desires, fears, and beliefs to die while you are yet alive. The experience of the loss of one's personal identity is indeed terrifying, yet it is the most rewarding of all the deaths that we shall die... and it is the only one that is everlasting. Thus, to attain complete liberation you must, at some point along your pathway, abandon or transmute the personal self which you and the world have falsely created, for it shields and clouds the truth of your ultimate reality. Then, once empty of this identity, will you begin to experience the fullness within you, and merge into that which is your true essence.

I will fly fly fly through eternity's sky
and spin into the pupil of my soul's eye.
A world beyond my most imaginative dream
where I am an ageless, rainbow light beam.

I fell out of the moonlit sky
like a teardrop sliding from an empty eye…
Tumbling across the sleeping sky
I woke and rose in dawn's eye.

I walked out of my house, stepped onto a branch, and flew out over the sea
to forget my identity, which I never really knew.

Do not cling to the moments of your life, but rather, experience to the fullest each moment of life by being aware of the present reality; and gracefully move with the moment as an artist of change.

Life is change.
All is ever-moving.
The Earth constantly turns
while flaming infinity burns
and water flows
water flows
water flows.
Movement
motion

movement
motion
movement
motion
is constant.

Meandering on the shores of Infinity, we dance on the moving arena of life and taste the sweet nectar of freedom.

As we rejoice amidst a sea of stars which float in everlasting silence, we glimpse our purpose.

The night won't let me sleep… the stars keep winking at me and the clouds keep whispering sweet words in my ears.

Goodnight, goodnight, goodnight…
May you sleep under a blanket of moonlight
and roll through the heavens
and rise with a glorious stretch
into dawn's first breath…

I woke this morning and stepped into the sunset to go to sleep.

Every human being has an inner connection to the animal world, a true family. I am from the bird tribe.

The truth of our existence is found amidst the lies of our culture. Underneath the enticing advertisements, the beautifully painted mazes of illusion, and the facades of our egos alluringly wrapped in the trends of the times—lies the essence of our existence.

Balance your consciousness on the tip of the pine needle. Meditate upon it. You are life's creative force; yield the power and use it at will. Anything is attainable.

Look! The seasons are spinning, the garden is blooming... before our very eyes. It never stops!

Soap opera society world,
fancy clothes, work disease...
I've had enough!
I don't want to wear shoes
or comb my hair,
I want to roam the earth
free and bare.

Our lives are lacking the passion and purpose that come from being in tune with the rhythms of nature.

Sometimes I wonder if the reason tree branches twist and turn in such fascinating ways is because they are stretching out, as we do upon rising each morning. Perhaps some trees are indeed engaged in a lifelong morning stretch.

Universal life stream… Universe, a life's dream…

Universes… u-niver-ses… you niver ses… you never cease…

Awareness… a war en ess… a war in us…
a war in us… aware in us… awareness…

Our lives are a ceaseless movement which lasts a single moment.

Creation is unceasing. Eternity is here. Forever is now. Breathe…

O blind one, how clearly you see the light of the sun.
O deaf one, how sharply you hear the sounds of nature.
O mute one, how perfectly you speak of the blue sky.
O wise one, may you know the ways of the blind, deaf, and mute.

Release me from the realm of words, thoughts, and emotions, so I may fly high in Spirit.

If you think you are taking the beauty of the air and the magic of breath for granted, abstain from breathing for a moment.

It is as cleansing and purifying for the mind to fast from thought as it is for the body to fast from food.

Anyplace, everyplace, yet no place is home for the Warrior of the Now.

Black night, vast sea, and endless sky inflict upon me my tininess.

It is true a picture can be worth a thousand words, but the right word can be worth a thousand pictures.

I petted a wild deer today along the shore of Lake Siskiyou.

Your time in this form, in this manner, is limited. Seize it!

A wish is a dream with longing... remote, unattainable. A dream is a wish made real in the timeless, infinite land of imagination.

A micro-universe thrives in each drop of water, in each grain of sand...

Within each instant, lies eternity.
Within each movement, lies stillness.
Within each sound, lies silence...
the uninterrupted, endless hum of silence.

Deep within the turning of the Earth is complete stillness.
Deep within the stillness of my being is endless motion.

Each and every one of us is a magical being made of earth, water, and light energy. We are all travelers of evolution connected to the infinite power source of the universe. Within us is the ability to heal ourselves, or make ourselves ill, to expand our consciousness, or waste it. This is the gift and the challenge of being human.

May the flame of life within you expand and flourish infinitely.

May life forever show you its magical beauty and marvelous unexpectedness.

On Poems and Words

Poems
are not simply words
but thoughts
ideas
clothed with feeling.
And if one of my poems
brings a smile
to the face of another,
and if one of my poems
brings a peaceful thought
to the mind of another,
then my friends,
my purpose has been achieved.

To a poet, a poem is a blossom.
New and fresh it is created.
And a poem is a fruit,
the poet being the tree.
Some fruits are eaten ripe
while others are left to rot into the earth.
And a poem when ripe, is a fruit
which can help living things grow
and live with purity and health.

Words…
sounds coming out of our mouths
organized noises
to which we attribute meaning…
they evoke images, spawn thought, and stir feelings.
Nothing more, nothing less.

You choose your reality
your pain your suffering your happiness your joy
chosen by your perceptions
chosen by your mind, your frame of consciousness.

These words I write
have different meanings to each of us
depending upon how we see life
and upon the meanings we have gathered
from our experiences here on earth.

This poem has nothing for you
but to offer you a reflection of yourself
these words are a mirror for you to look into your mind
and see who you are…
Nothing more, nothing less.

Conversation with an Elder

A Native American elder came to speak at our school today. I met with him in the auditorium after his presentation to the children…

"You are a teacher here?" he inquired.

"Yes," I replied, and introduced myself.

"I have observed the school quite thoroughly," he began. "Strangely, the young children play in a concrete yard, surrounded by metal fences. I find it to be similar to your society's prison yards. Are the children being punished?" he asked.

"No," I answered, "but that's an interesting comparison. The playground fences are designed just as much to keep others out, as to keep the children in."

"Hmm. I see," he responded. "But where are the trees? How can the children learn without trees? How can they play without grass or natural earth?"

There was a moment of silence between us while I thought about his question and what my response would be.

"I am told," he continued, "that at most of the schools, the children learn entirely indoors, in specially designed rectangular rooms. Is that correct?"

"For the most part," I replied.

"I'm confused," he said. "How can the children learn about life on Earth indoors? How can they learn about respect and truth without plants and trees?"

Again there was silence between us. On many levels, I shared his concerns.

"Many of your culture's children," he said, "are sick, confused, angry, disturbed. What will become of the future if the children are not taught the truth and knowledge of nature? What will become of our world if the children are products of computers, indoor rooms, and concrete yards bound by tall metal fences?"

I had no response, no bright answer, for I realized that ultimately I agreed with him. I hummed a muted syllable, something like, "Mmm."

"You have work to do, Marsh," he said. "It's time for your people to awaken. It will soon be too late. You must begin to teach the truth, not virtual illusions…"

On Independent Thinking

Have not inflexible allegiance to procedure, but rather consider function first. Practice love before rules, for there is always a higher purpose. Consider practicality over regulation; human beings are not robots. Take the initiative to think for yourself and make individual decisions with compassion and kindness. We are each conscious beings with the ability to create the world we live in. Take heed that ye may not surrender your individual authority. Take heed that ye may not submit your life and destiny to the hands of human law and false rulers. Stand firm in your ability to question the established way. Stand firm in your ability and right to make decisions for yourself. Be flexible beyond human rule. Remember higher purposes apply to every situation, every act, every word, every deed, and every thought. If you surrender your sense of individuality and your ability to make decisions beyond the scope of regulation, you surrender your own human beingness. And lastly, always let love, truth, compassion, and kindness guide you...

Whoops

I woke and wandered west with the warming wind. Weaving my way through wafting weeds, I willfully withdrew my worries, whirling them away from the world where they would no longer cause me to whine or whimper.

One who worships the wind is a wizard. A wizard will not worry, but wonder. A wise wizard whistles with the wings of the air. A warrior on the wild path wields wisdom as well. The wide-eyed, white-haired, weathered wizard whispers wherever the wind will wheel him, always welcoming water. Water will wash away one's woes.

So I walked westward with the wind and whirled through weeds and willows while whistling at the wild world with the wolves, until my wayward route wound me to a whitewash of wet whirling waves. Whoops, I almost forget, it was a Wednesday, in winter…

On the Sun and the Sea

When the Sun spins and sings its song of colors, and my mind seeps into gentle waves of motion... I will flow with the Sea.

I sing to the sun and ride ocean waves to the land of bliss.

O to drink the sound of the turquoise Pacific crashing onto a sandy stretch of California. O to swim through the blue sky and roll across warm rays of sunshine.

May the soft smile of the ocean stir the embers of your soul.

The ocean is forever making sand... and life moves about in its rhythm.

Every afternoon the western horizon beckons me with a fleeting path of gleaming golden sunshine glistening on the smooth sea. Sometimes I embark upon this path, but never do I get far; for by dusk the path has faded into the deep hues of twilight and is gone. Perhaps someday I will walk its lengths unto Eternity.

Let the sea dissolve all that is hard within you.
Let it polish you into your fineness
and nourish you into your ripeness.
Let it breathe its perfection into you.

Tonight
as I rode the ocean
I could feel
the golden light
of dusk's warm glow.
It softened my mind, my being, my world
and melted away the ripples of the day.
I feel like a pelican.

Sea for Yourself

Sea the earth
as a brilliant speck
in a vast universe

Sea the ocean
as a drop of dew
on a flower's petal

Sea yourself
as a tiny ripple
reflecting the sun's love

Ocean Essence

Crashing foam
shimmering blues and greens
perfect power
aaah…

Who Am I?

I am the power of the wild, raging storm and I am the power of the still, silent morning.

I am a leaf on the branch of a tree in the forest, whose roots stretch deep into the sacred earth and limbs reach tall into the limitless sky.

I am not me. I am a spark of Spirit shining through a six-foot speck of dust.

I am a tender of the crops and a keeper of the green, a server of the light and a part of the force unseen.

Am I a thinker, or an ignorant fool? Am I a poet, or an idiot? Do I write poems, or just nonsense?

I am electricity...
Current...
Darting across eons of open sky...
Free in the wind.

I am a stray being, a wanderer on a blooming sphere whirling through space. I am a nomad, roaming the face of a mysterious round world that spins through the skies.

I am fueled with the energy of my Father. I am blazing with the light of my Mother.

I am a gatherer of power… God power! I am a harmonizer with the energy of the universe.

Who am I? I am you, and you are me, and we are all This. So look around… at each other. Look around… at yourself.

I come from a clan of great soul warriors, of elders who possess ancient wisdom and powerful, naturally-harmonized energy. I am a soul rider, a liquid cosmos glider… from the bird tribe. Long live the bird tribe!

Part Fourteen

The Heart of a Traveler

Alive

I am free...
as I wander the wide deserts of earth...
amidst the ocotillo, the cholla, and the great cardón.

I am free...
under the blazing sun...
on lost mountaintops seldom visited by humans.

I am free...
as beads of sweat trickle down my sun-weathered face.

I am free...
as turkey vultures soar high above the distant, unnamed peaks...
weightless in the sea of blue sky.

I am free...
in my thoughts, in my mind,
anywhere, everywhere, always, and forever.

I am alive...
and my spirit flourishes.

--Central Desert of Baja California, Mexico, 1993

An Agent of Peace

I am an agent of peace
walking a path bright and strong.
Bravely I walk
true to nature.
I cannot be corrupted
nor can I be tamed
by greed.
I am an agent of nature's peace
alive and charged with its sheer, raw purity
and power.
Free.
Loving life
treasuring earth.
Join me…

The Ends of the Earth (Finale)

We have journeyed long,
this my brother and I.
To the ends of the earth we have come.
As the prehistoric land calls me back,
I smile softly to myself
beneath the blazing sun.
And I know, regardless of how harshly life shakes me,
no matter how much my shell crumbles
I will endure and thrive
and ultimately flourish.
For be it in living or be it in dying,
I am the power of the stars and sea,
and I am eternal.

--Punta Canoas, Baja California, Mexico, 1996

Author's Note: Punta Canoas lies in perhaps the most isolated region of Central Baja California's Pacific coast. Due to its geographical position and its extreme distance from the solitary paved road which traverses the peninsula, the journey to Canoas consists of long hours upon dusty dirt roads through wild desert landscapes. The trip, like most Baja traveling, is arduous and dangerous. The traveler must carry all necessities and provisions, including water, food, extra gas, and medical supplies. The roads are terrible, the hazards are numerous, and the outcome is always uncertain. Help and assistance can often be impossible to find. The reward for such a journey is an intrinsic one, and is ultimately in the journey itself. However, if you reach Canoas and remain there for any significant duration, you will experience firsthand some of the most stunning and majestic, yet barren coastal terrain in the world, where the harsh, untamed desert meets the blue Pacific. Beyond this, you will likely find yourself forever changed, and emerge from the journey with a fresh feeling of distance from who you've previously believed yourself to be. This, friends, is the beginning of the discovery of who you really are. Yes, and if you're really blessed, you may even score some great point surf. Special thanks to my old friend and fellow surf-adventurer, Jason Appleton, for accompanying me on this and many other incredible Baja journeys.

Only for a Moment

Some down time at La Duna…
women gather
working quietly with clay
fashioning curious thoughts and wafting emotions
into form.
They sit
you sit
circle-patterned in the palapa
like ancient native weavers.
I sit
silently, reflectively
in your hut
atop your bed
where you lay
where you sleep
where you breathe…
where we have met and chatted
and explored sharing space
with the most delicate and careful sense
of that marginally magical and most interesting word—
discernment.

Outside the hut
our clothing and swimsuits hang out to dry.
They dance together
in hot desert winds.
Inside
water bottles and glasses
mirror
on opposing counter tops

while bags and clothes
intermingle.
Our boots rest together on the floor.
They could get used to this, they tell me.
Somehow it seems so easy
so harmonious
so perfect
so possible
so "natural"
so close…

Savor this, lovely friend
for it will soon be gone…
like a shooting star burning through the darkness
or the flicker of a firefly in the night…
or the break of dawn before a beautiful, fiery goddess
her slender figure dropped deep into warrior pose…
A man's tent nearby…
together overlooking the spectacle of new birth
new day
rising sun
fading night.

This that we have shared is not an illusion*
nor is it a dream
but the momentarily fused mind and heart
of warrior and goddess
king and queen
man and woman
embraced
in that long, undefinable, before-bed hug,
tucked carefully inside the hut
beneath the mystical shelter
of whirling

illuminated
dark
vast
cosmos.

Across the valley
in nearby canyons void of humans
vultures sit atop tall cardón
and scurrying mice halt and shudder
overcome with the power of echoing drum rhythms
and distant voices raised in song.
The sound waves travel onward...
A sea lion pup twirls in the hidden darkness
of her underwater cave.
She surfaces,
lifts her head above the sea
and gazes briefly at twinkling starlight.
She too hears the rhythms
and the faint voices of her relatives.
She flashes upon the odd, masked, pale
god and goddess
who held and caressed her
one auspicious afternoon...

Night winds blow stronger now,
desert shrubs rattle...
a horse calls out,
another joins in.
Images flash through their strong minds
of running along beaches,
the pale beings upon their backs.
The rhythms still pulse
GA DUN KA TA
GA DUN KA TA

through lost canyons
over now abandoned windswept dunes
beyond sparkling sea
beyond sky and soaring cloud
beyond sun...
permeating flesh
bone
sangre
wet lips and thumping heart...

Savor this, beautiful woman
for it will soon be gone...
the sacred heart stone from your secret cove
rests now
and only for a moment
upon your pillow.

--Baja California, Mexico, October 2010

*Author's Note: * This line was inspired by the poem "This We Have Now" by the great thirteenth-century Persian poet and Sufi mystic, Jelaluddin Rumi, known commonly as Rumi. "This we have now is not imagination" is the opening line.*

Traveler's Song from the Windswept Plain

Verse I

Loneliness is a cruel beast
which eats away at me
feeding itself on my living heart
leaving me with a large empty space
a gap
a hole in my heart
that bleeds all over everything.
And the further I journey
deeper into the mountains
of this magical desert
where few humans have ever traveled
where no humans exist
deeper into the Spirit world
alone
where my only companion is my shadow
and my only answer an echo
the beast gorges itself,
eating voraciously of my heart…

But in this hole, in this void,
in this gaping bloody wound
something greater is being placed
by a power far beyond my comprehension.
And with each step of my journey
across these ancient lands,
the golden dust of the desert
fills the void.
And as I gaze

at the endless sea of mountains
which await,
they fulfill me with something greater
than anything I have ever known…

And as the beast of loneliness struggles
for its feeble existence,
the magic, the mystery, the power
of the unknown, the unexplainable,
the beauty of this life
permeates everything I am…
until I am One…
never to be the same again.
And my being glows with this magic.

Verse II

I am not like those people…
I am a fluke.
I am like a broken spoke
in the wheel of society.
I don't live like them, think like them, act like them,
feel like them, eat like them, dress like them…
I am a modern-day mystic
a soul explorer, a solo traveler
living a life very different
than that of the mainstream.
I can co-exist with them
but only for short spans
until my journeys call me away again
to the timeless lands of the world
which I love so much…
a different world, a different existence,
a different reality.

Yes, I am like the broken spoke
in the wheel of humanity...
but it is not the brokenness
of hurt, pain, or distress,
it is more like the beauty
of one who is free and unrestrained...
unbound by the mental and physical
chains of society,
and wholeheartedly following
the path of the soul...

This... Now

This...
walking across these rocks...
is all I know,
and all I ever shall know.
This...
walking across these rocks.

This...
riding upon this wave...
is all I know,
and all I ever shall now.
This...
riding upon this wave.

This...
gazing into the setting sun...
is all I know,
and all I ever shall know.
This...
gazing into the setting sun.

This...
now...
nothing else.

--Eternity (Experienced at North Beacon's, Leucadia,
California, Planet Earth, January 31, 2017)

Four the Divine

Thank you Ocean for cleansing me.
Thank you Sun for warming me.
Thank you Earth for comforting me.
Thank you Spirit for providing me.

Shadow Self in the Crystal Fields, a self-portrait, version two, Central Baja California, Mexico, overlooking the Sea of Cortez. Photo by the author.

The Heart of a Traveler:
A Morning Near El Tomatal

As the faint breath of dawn begins to glow in the eastern sky
we rise slowly and pack up our sleeping gear...
In silence
we make our way, in my truck,
through a network of sandy dirt roads
amidst the barren coastal environment of Central Baja—
sparse chaparral and assorted cacti.
The salt air wafts in a light breeze
carrying the scent of the sea...
it swirls around us
mixing with the dust kicked up by my truck.

After a time, we reach the paved highway,
the narrow band where wanderers roam from north to south
and back again
looking for their own answers
their own reasons.
The Mexican army has set up camp with tarps and machine guns.
They stop us for a short while, looking for drugs and weapons.
Most of them are quite young—nineteen or twenty years-old—
maybe younger.
They are curious about the two scruffy gringo surfers before them.

This was a morning filled with omens
signs
which those who journey must be aware of,
although we'd likely ignore them nonetheless
considering our level of intensity
and commitment to the adventure.

It was the day of our life-changing accident
only we did not know it yet.
The old Spanish church in the oasis village of San Ignacio
would hint it to us later that afternoon
with faded images of a wounded Christ adorning the ancient walls.

Oh yes, the omens...
As we continued south that early morning
winding down Baja's infamous Highway 1,
roaming deeper into the desert wilderness
through ever more desolate regions of the semi-abandoned peninsula,
a bobcat skirted across our path.
She was young, not yet fully grown
and thin—
it's a hard life even for a bobcat
in such challenging terrain.
She ran weakly through the dry, waterless landscape,
disappearing from our sight amidst clumps of cholla cactus
and brittle shrubs.

Next there was a beautiful yellow bird
that appeared from seemingly nowhere
as we were temporarily stopped by the roadside.
She landed atop a cactus a mere few feet away
and looked at us curiously...
as if she had come to pay her respects
or wish us well on our journey...
or glimpse us before we vanish into the unknown
or depart from the world.
She left in a sudden flutter as quickly as she had come.

There was a third omen,
a grotesque happening in the rundown town of Guerrero Negro.
It was too horrendous for us to discuss in any duration—

the fresh blood of a pup,
who moments before we watched trotting along happily,
was spilled across the filthy street by an oblivious driver.
He ignored the brief cry and thump
and drove onward unconcernedly in his old Ford pick-up
as the sacred, beautiful life of an ownerless, nameless young dog
came to a harsh, abrupt end in the dirt and dust of this little Mexican town.

Thus there were questions
buried deep in our minds
beneath layers of emotion,
kicked up by the profound sorrow now swirling in the breeze
and made obvious and apparent by the shock and horror of death.
It brewed into an overwhelming mixture of awe and fear
before the natural and unnatural elements of this world...
before the pain, desperation, and suffering
that is both inescapable and unavoidable
in our lives.
We existed momentarily in a state of mind
of being
where excitement and hopelessness coexisted...
where life and death convened.
It was infinity and finality all at once...
eternity and impermanence flaunting themselves simultaneously
before us, around us, within us...
There was no turning back
no safe harbor
no shelter from the wind
no going home.

These varying, polarized elements
so very true and real in all of our lives
challenged, opposed, and threatened one another,
and each of us

as those unwelcomed questions rose to the surface of our minds
like they often do in our most vulnerable moments.
They were the same questions that often haunt the adventurer
who journeys deep into the enigmatic realm of unfamiliarity
of solitude
or anyone who ventures into the unknown
far away from his or her common, comfortable
and deceptively safe reality,
and these are:
What do these experiences mean?
What are the signs, the warnings,
and how should we respond or alter our course because of them?
Will anyone know that we were here—
in this time
in this land
to see these things which no other eyes have seen
or ever will see?
Will we ever return home?
Will we see our loved ones again?
Will we die down here, so far away from home?

Yet in the midst of such intense questioning
there's an indistinct security
an ephemeral peace
an almost imperceptible sense of universal connection
a deep stillness felt and experienced in the powerful silence
of the vast landscape.
This sense of well-being
of oneness
of surrender
forms the basic core,
the heart
of the traveler,
the journeying one.

This *is* my home,
here
in this land
at this time
and if I die in it
I die *well*,
for this universe
this cosmos
our cosmos
on a whole
is beneficent.
Regardless of what happens
here
or wherever my journeys take me,
our universe
and thus its life, *my* life, *your* life
is a beautiful and glorious one...
and I am grateful to have lived and experienced it
in such fullness.
Yes, if I die now,
I die not in hunger, nor in longing, nor in sadness
but in satiation
in peace
in fulfillment.

--Central Desert, Baja California, Mexico, June 2001

Dissolution into Salt

I trod westward across the sands
toward the cold blue waters of the Pacific...
My feet crunch upon countless broken seashells,
colored pieces of life now departed.
Still vibrant—even beautiful—
yet the life that was once there is gone.

And so I enter into sea...
others surround me yet I am alone...
and I toss pain aside... into sea
I toss suffering aside... into sea
I toss failure aside...
even success I toss aside... into sea.

I toss joy and happiness aside... into sea
I toss sadness aside... into sea
I toss loneliness and longing aside...
even fulfillment I cast away... into sea.

I toss sorrow aside... into sea
I toss pride aside... into sea
and finally, at last
I toss even identity aside... into sea...
until at last I am only death...
total dissolution into water and salt.
And in this dissolving
this dying
only life remains...

Sojourns of a Stranger

Dawn broke early
this brisk, icy morn.
The sun rose brightly
over the eastern coast
over Neptune's Atlantic waters.
Last night
I traveled in my dreams
across this grand continent
over the Appalachians
and through the heartland.
I soared freely
in my silver dream body
over the wide, star-filled deserts of Texas,
New Mexico, Arizona.
I glided over the Sierras
to reach the grand Pacific,
my homeland,
if such a place exists for me upon this wild earth.
There the falling moon
setting below the western horizon
beckoned me with a path
of dancing white light upon dark ocean,
calling me further away from land
to water
only to water.

Further I flew,
across the placid Pacific,
following the moon's path into some remote region of eternity,
into some strange aspect of myself.

"Come, child,
come home," Spirit called.
"But where is home?" I asked.
Spirit, moon, light, presence,
drew me further out over the waters
away from familiarity
until suddenly the moon set
dipping below that ever-unreachable western horizon
and dropping out of my sight.
The sky grew dark
only a faint orange trace remained,
the dying glow of the traveling gypsy moon.

Goddesses have come to me
they abide for a time
we sit together
bedazzled
looking into each other's eyes...
I treasure these moments
however fleeting they may be
when lifetimes are consumed
and identities gained and lost
in love...

Goddesses have come to me
I notice always
their overpowering beauty
their beaming eyes
the light shining from their faces
the love pouring out through their smiles...
They bring to me a temporary comfort
a momentary sense of peace and happiness
but they always leave...

Thus I am alone
to walk this strange path
in this unknown land.
And my heart is filled with music,
the music of love
and longing,
it pours through me,
bleeding onto the world wherever I move.

And the Goddesses will continue to come
to sit with me
to watch me
to talk with me
to sing with me…
They pass like floating leaves
vanish like rare flowers,
leaving sweet fragrances like jasmine in their wakes.

So I journey onward
with only that distant, inner music to guide me…
I know not where…

Silhouette of a man at twilight, Medicine Lake, Northern California. Photo by Linda Lobbestael.

Epilogue:
Beings of the Void

꜏

A *void* is an empty space, a gap, or an opening. According to modern astronomical science, the void is the empty space between the planets, moons, stars, and even between the galaxies. In fact, this emptiness, referred to as space, outer space, or even intergalactic space, makes up the majority of the universe. Our own solar system consists almost entirely of space. Astronomical science tells us, however, that this great cosmic void is not completely empty, but "consists of a hard vacuum containing a low density of particles, predominantly a plasma of hydrogen and helium as well as electromagnetic radiation, magnetic fields, neutrinos, dust and cosmic rays" (Outer space, Wikipedia). What does this mean to us as human beings? What practical knowledge does this information provide us, if any? If we delve deeply into this concept, it can be argued that the universe is incredibly desolate in its nature… and yet somehow in this gigantic, immeasurable emptiness, we have come to be. Perhaps, even more importantly, the infinite void of intergalactic space is not only where we come from, but ultimately, who we are. We are beings of the void…

Verse I

The void…
that mysterious place within
where the lines of heartbeat and neural impulses converge
where we experience profound, beautiful connection
and yet the darkness and grief of separation.
The void…
our inner link to the outer cosmos.

Verse II

The void…
the subconscious sense
that we are sentient beings on a spherical planet
whirling through an unknown galaxy
a massive realm of light, stellar explosions, stardust, meteoritic debris
a vast cosmos filled with endless darkness and glowing celestial brilliance.

Verse III

This is our home, our reality, where we are, who we are…
Our comfortable living rooms and incessant televised entertainment
are but a temporary facade, a technological illusion
a momentary distraction
for we are beings of the void, you and I…
beings of this marvelous, mysterious, terrifying, immense
beautiful cosmic void…

References

Baba, Meher. *Not We but One*. Bombay, India: Meher House Publication, 1977. Print.

"Bottlenose dolphin." *en.wikipedia.org*. Wikipedia, n.d. Web. 20 Nov. 2016.

"Dissolution." *merriam-webster.com*. Merriam-Webster, Incorporated, 2015. Web. 13 July 2015.

"Edge." *merriam-webster.com*. Merriam-Webster, Incorporated, 2015. Web. 18 Jan. 2016.

Grimm D., & Miller, G. (2010, February 21). Is a Dolphin a Person? *Science*, *327*(5969), 1070-1071. Retrieved from http://www.sciencemag.org/news/2010/02/dolphin-person

Marsh, Ari. *Sea-Soaked Heart: Thoughts from the Pacific Coast*. Leucadia, CA: Soul Rider Publications, 2004. Print.

-------. *Smiling at the Sun: Ways of the Golden Path*. Leucadia, CA: Soul Rider Publications, 1991. Print.

-------. *The Soul Rider: A Surfer's Perspective of the World*. Leucadia, CA: Soul Rider Publications, 1992. Print.

-------. *The Soul Rider II: Neptune's Dream*. Leucadia, CA: Soul Rider Publications, 1995. Print.

-------. *The Voice of Eternity: A Book of Aphorisms*. Leucadia, CA: Soul Rider Publications, 1993. Print.

"Outer space." *en.wikipedia.org.* Wikipedia, n.d. Web. 31 Dec. 2015.

Random House Webster's College Dictionary. 2d ed. New York: Random House, 2000. Updated annually. Print.

Rumi, Jelaluddin. *The Essential Rumi.* Trans. Coleman Barks. New York: HarperCollins, 1995. Print.

Waters, Frank. *The Man Who Killed the Deer.* Athens: Ohio University Press, 1985. Print.

Index

About the Author

Ari Marsh is a writer, poet, world musician, and global adventurer born and raised in Southern California. He holds a Bachelor of Arts degree in Communication from San Diego State University and a Master of Education from National University. Throughout his life, he has traveled to some twenty countries, immersing himself in the sacred places of Mexico, Peru, Israel, India, Japan, Italy, France, Spain, and Indonesia. His previous book, *Echoes from the Sun: A Modern Quest for the Fountain of Youth*, is a spiritual adventure and the culmination of more than a decade of research and global exploration. It continues to soar on Amazon with 5-Star reviews. Both *Echoes* and *The Heart of a Traveler: Reflections from the Fathomless Edge of the World* are available on Amazon in paperback and Kindle. As today's literary marketplace is increasingly based upon customer feedback, please take a moment to review this book on Amazon and other relevant sites. Ari's writings and music can be further explored at www.AriMarsh.com and www.echoesfromthesun.com.

Behold! A new journey from Ari Marsh has begun…

"Remarkable! An astounding spiritual odyssey!"
"A MUST READ for anyone on any sort of spiritual journey."
"Written absolutely beautifully!"

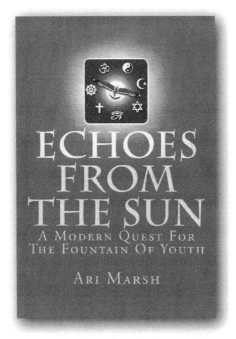

In the mountains of Mexico a solo traveler has discovered an ancient amulet believed to hold mysterious powers that can heal disease and prolong life, possibly changing the course of humanity, rewriting history, ending centuries of war, and uniting people of all faiths. The quest to explore its powers leads this brave, solitary adventurer on a worldwide journey into the secret mysteries of life that bind us together at our core and fuse us with the limitless energy of the cosmos.

Now available in paperback and Kindle through Amazon.com
and other retailers.
ISBN-13: 978-1466454897

www.echoesfromthesun.com

82425731R00240

Made in the USA
Columbia, SC
17 December 2017